AF281319

This book focuses on different manifestations of polarization. They show up between:
- abundance and hunger
- wealth and poverty
- sufficient and no longer sufficient resources like raw materials, energy, and environment.

Before considering central concepts of polarization, a first stage of the development of polarization must be explained. It is characterized, among other things, by the fact that people often receive different incomes. This creates an incentive for people with lower incomes to earn higher incomes. As a result, the real economy can experience growth. Furthermore, different variations of polarization are shown as well as polarization with its relations to other terms.

- Societal polarization is characterized by the fact that incomes and wealth of parts of the population drift so far apart that malnutrition and abundance or poverty and wealth can arise. Such a development is driven by excessive asymmetric and thus also percental distribution of growth gains. Such a development is driven by excessive asymmetric and thus also percental distribution of growth gains.

- Global polarization is evident between countries Excessive differences in the trade balances cause, among other things the differences between the countries.

- Ecological polarization can be seen between the times of still sufficient or already too low resource reserves of raw materials, energy, and environment.

- Polarization and its relationship to democracy: There are approaches which, within democratic states, focus on the real economic satisfaction of the people involved and on securing their future through sustainability. The following approaches are intended to reduce polarization: Limiting existential differences, recycling, providing renewable energy and environmental protection.

- Polarization and its relationship to resource reserves: Many people who receive low compensation for their products or low incomes tend to remain poor. Thus, they can do little to diminish the resource reserves. For the richer people, resources then last longer. These people benefit from polarization.

- Polarization and its relationship to authoritarian leadership: Some states move toward authoritarian leadership when there is polarization between the poorer and the richer parts of the population. This can happen as follows: When negative polarization effects occur among the poorer people, the beneficiaries logically try to ensure stability with the help of authoritarian leadership.

- Polarization-reducing activities often do not sufficiently take place in the context of polarization. This is because many rich states can cast out the consequences of polarization such as hunger and poverty, which they have contributed to, with the help of oceans, fences and walls and thus, directly combatting polarization is partly unnecessary for them. Furthermore, rich countries benefit from the poverty of other countries because the latter can consume relatively few resources and thus the resource consumption horizon of rich countries is enlarged. The climate and oceans occupy a special position because the consequences of their consumption and pollution largely ignore borders. In this context, environmental degradation may continuously take place, accompanied by economic, technical and militant constellations.

This book illuminates polarizing influences, their consequences, and possible ways to mitigate them.

Guenter Polhede

Polarization

societal

global

ecological

2024-05-26

Polarization – societal, global, ecological
Guenter Polhede, E-Mail: gpolhede@yahoo.de

Bibliographic information of the German National Library:
The German National Library lists this publication in the German
National Bibliography; detailed bibliographic data are available on
the Internet at dnb.dnb.de.

Production and Publishing:
BoD – Books on Demand, Norderstedt / Germany

ISBN 9783759758453

Translated by: **ms**übersetzungen Marion Spreen,
                   Rahden/Germany

Illustrated by: Stefanie Zech

2024-05-26

Table of contents

Table of contents Page

Table of contents   Page

Table of contents   Page

Table of contents   Page

Table of contents

Table of contents Page

Table of contents   Page

Table of contents

Table of contents   Page

Table of contents   Page

Table of contents		Page

A   Overview

A 1   Overview – Key points

The terms capitalism, economic growth, and consumption play an important role in societal discussions. They are starting points for criticism of social conditions. The criticism states that there are people who have too much money, who have too much economic growth to answer for, or who realize too much consumption. It is a description of differences between presumed normal conditions and deviating conditions which are therefore criticized. These deviations can be called polarization, as far as they assume large dimensions. For this purpose, some introductory considerations shall be made.

If quantitative real economic growth is initiated by a continuous demand for goods, the consumption and investment goods obtained in the process are paid for out of growth successes, i.e., wages, salaries, and profits.

If growth gains cannot be realized to such an extent that the expectations of all participants can be met, the realization of expectations of one part of the population often takes place at the expense of another part of the population.

Desired growth is also achieved to a certain extent at the expense of dwindling resources.

The above-mentioned negative developments already show that polarization can arise, represented by poverty and wealth, hunger and abundance, and varying degrees of access to diminishing resource reserves. There are polarizations within societies and between countries. To this end, a sophisticated approach is required.

If humans had to arrange their life only with their hands labor, they would exhaust their time and strength entirely. However, in the

course of time, people have acquired reinforcing factors, among other things by using
- applied education
- energy
- raw materials
- machinery
- information technology

Reinforcing factors enable people to live their lives increasingly well. With its use, quantitative real economic growth can be driven to the benefit of many people. To break down real economic growth, the following variables are considered:
- goods
- labor
- current account surplus
- waste of goods, e.g., food
- resources such as energy, raw materials, and environment
- innovative products
- status symbols
- recycling and renewable energy
- investments
- education
- savings and loans
- redistribution for community projects

If growth benefits are distributed in a highly asymmetrical manner to the people involved, societal and even global polarizations are initially possible.

These variants of polarization can facilitate a splitting of the financial market, into a real economic and a speculative part. The break-up takes place, for example, if more and more people accumulate so much money that they do not only use it for real economic purposes, but also for speculative ones.

If the speculative part of the financial market increases significantly, confidence in the stability of the value of money can be weakened to an excessive degree. Once the confidence in the value of money as an information carrier, together with its associated information, becomes too low, the question arises whether money ca be replaced by other information carriers and information.

Social or global polarization represent the first types of polarization. The people involved benefit very differently from the growth achievements on the goods markets.

The first variants of polarization can generate another one. This is the ecological variant. This is driven by resource consumption and is thus located in the ecological sphere. It can be imagined emerging between two points in time as follows.

The more people participate in growth gains on the goods markets, the more this growth can be at the expense of resource reserves of raw materials, energy, and the environment as a result of the accompanying resource consumption. For the ecological variation of polarization driven by resource consumption, we can assume an original state of sufficient resource reserves. With increasing resource consumption, these can become scarce and even too scarce. The ecological polarization driven by resource consumption can be seen in the stage of scarcity, in which parts of the population or countries have a decreasing access to some resources. The stage of scarcity becomes critical if the resource reserves have been irreversibly diminished to such an extent that they are no longer sufficiently available for all people. This process particularly affects the environment.

This is the background to a complex analysis of the polarization driven by an asymmetric distribution of growth gains or by resource consumption:

-      It becomes evident that, regarding social and global polarization, there are beneficiaries and disadvantaged people whose roles must be differentiated.

- In competition with other people, polarization initially motivates them to achieve as much growth gains as the others. However, in the course of time, and in the case of asymmetric distribution of growth gains, this process generates not only wealth but also poverty.

- Furthermore, real economic growth tends to result in too much environmental consumption over time.

- Some people, as beneficiaries of the different variations of polarization, obviously have an interest in ignoring or even denying the negative consequences for people disadvantaged by this development.

- The analysis attempts to find out how negative consequences of the different variations of polarization and their explosive social effects can be limited.

- On the one hand, the analysis examines the extent to which different types of polarization can be reduced by redistribution and, on the other hand, the extent to which democratically legitimized groups of individuals acting via information technology could act via depolarization.

- Furthermore, the analysis will focus on the extent to which the sustainable use of resources, such as renewable energy, recycling and environmental protection can significantly reduce ecological polarization.

A 2   Overview – All individuals are on a global staircase of competition – among other things between hunger and abundance

Fairy tales about the future might start like this:
Once upon a time all people
- had enough to drink and eat,
- lived in warm and dry conditions,
- had their diseases treated as well as possible,
- could afford reasonable comfort,
- had enough money to pay for it,
- had sufficiently paid work,
- consumed resources only to the extent that they would be sufficient in the long run,
- consumed the environment only to the extent that it could adequately regenerate itself,
- … And then, there were hardly any occasions for polarization between rich and poor, hunger and abundance and between conditions like still enough or already too little environment, which provoke conflicts of distribution.

However, the reality shows that polarization does exist. There are for instance countries with many poor and few rich people, with rather poor and rather rich people or as well with many relatively rich and few relatively poor people. Polarization is not only visible within countries, but also globally between countries. To start with, polarization is discussed in the context of the phenomena concerning the real economy.

–   Polarization as an interaction of real economic growth, automation, rationalization and asymmetric distribution of income.

In an early stage of real economic development, human labor primarily is used to produce goods. These are the goods that people themselves want to use, sell, and buy. Human labor is also used to implement automation and rationalization to produce more goods to fulfil further needs.

The money paid for the use of human labor can be used to buy manufactured goods. If production and income increase continuously with the help of automation and rationalization, then a quantitative real economic growth is achieved.

At this point the idea must be mentioned that incomes like wages and salaries most of the time increase asymmetrically. A special form of this is the percentual increase. People with high incomes receive a higher amount as a supplement than people with low incomes.

The people who are needed for automation and rationalization, for example, may earn well - and make savings.

Over time, fewer people are needed to produce goods due to automation and rationalization and, as a result, they tend to receive less money.

The real economic cycle may receive too little money due to savings and too little earnings.

Thus, if there is a decrease in consumption, a decrease in demand and an oversupply of goods and human labor, people may become unemployed or earn less. Accordingly, such people can buy less and the demand will decrease. Real economic growth may weaken because of the self-reinforcing weakening of the demand.

There are still poor countries in which many people barely receive enough money for a decent life.

Obviously, everyone is part of a development that is characterized by polarization within and between countries.

Next, the ecological polarization driven by resource consumption is considered.

–   On a symbolic global staircase - competition - reinforcing factors - resource consumption - ecological polarization

All people on earth can be imagined on a symbolic staircase. There are starving people and those who live in as well as very poor and very rich people. The number of hungry, abundant, poor, and rich people and the degree of hunger, abundance, poverty and wealth are very different within different countries as well as between the countries.

People on the stairs are competing. They are competing for survival, some comfort, prosperity and ultimately probably for status and power. People try to enhance their labor force with the help of education, technical progress, machinery, automation, rationalization, energy, raw materials, and information technology. They get themselves a reinforcement factor and strive to increase it continuously.

In doing so, they hope to produce more and more goods for use and sale, to earn more and to be able to afford more.

The human reinforcement factor, however, is not only used to produce more and more goods, but in parallel to this, more and more resources such as energy, raw materials, and the environment are consumed. In this respect, competition as a driver of real economy destroys its basis if too many resources are consumed. This applies first to the resource "environment". There are two decisive states where the so-called ecological polarization takes place. State 1 means that there is still enough environment available. State 2, its consumption has progressed to such an extent that human existence may be irreversibly endangered on a global scale.

–   Interest groups and conflicts of distribution

In summary, automation and rationalization in combination with asymmetric distribution of growth benefits such as income are a driver for polarization. During this development, the gap between poverty and wealth and between hunger and abundance widens.

If, in response to this kind of development, the growth gains are distributed rather equally among all participants, then, unlike the asymmetric distribution of the growth gains, the poorer people receive larger supplements and the richer people receive smaller supplements. The poorer people then have more money for consumption and driving the real economy and indirectly for resource consumption and resource depletion. The richer people then have less money to save and thus to withdraw from the real economy cycles. If the poorer people, with more equal distribution of growth gains, substantially increase global resource consumption, the period of resource availability decreases for everyone involved, including the rich people.

Thus, it is obvious for the rather rich people to weaken the poor people financially, in terms of consumption possibilities and resource consumption, to extend the period in which there are still sufficient resources for themselves.

In this context, the real economic development shows that there are many people struggling for a minimum standard of living and whose way on the global staircase does not lead upwards, but often downwards. Many people in the world never have a chance in their life to leave the lowest steps of the stairs in the struggle for survival. Potential trouble spots form, accompanied by distribution fights, distribution wars and flight.

Parallel to this, there are also the people who climb the global staircase to a higher standard of living, to more income and to more wealth, thus climbing the staircase and increasing the polarization-driven tensions.

In this book, points of view are elaborated that show the tension between hunger and abundance, very poor and very rich, resource consumption and sustainability, or between environmental protection and environmental consumption. These aspects could improve transparency for individuals, groups, societies, countries, and states. Perhaps a slightly different development can be encouraged in this way to reduce polarization-related conflicts, fights and wars.

A 3   Overview - From the individual to securing resources

This passage covers the following concepts: Individual - democracy - sufficient economic growth - stable state - deficient economic growth - securing resources.

- Individual and society
- Democracy and community tasks
- Real economy, competition, and secrecy
- Quantitative real economic growth and community tasks
- Economy of growth - building bridges between real economy, democracy, and stable state
- Lack of growth gains and resource reserves

- Individual and society

Every individual is also part of a society. As a social actor, he or she plays a role in shaping society. All actors together change society. The behavior of individual actors continuously readjusts to the outcome of their aggregated activities.

Despite the complexity of the interaction between individuals and society, this book attempts to synthesize the interplay of individual satisfaction with the real economy, democracy, and state stability into a single conceptual framework.

In doing so, it illuminates how individual, real economic and democratic activities interact. This analysis is particularly carried out under the aspects of so-called sufficient quantitative real economic growth on the one hand and so-called insufficient quantitative real economic growth on the other hand.

There is sufficient quantitative growth in the real economy if almost all people who are capable of working have enough work and make enough money to live adequately. Quantitative real economic growth is considered to be deficient if such conditions do not exist for a substantial part of the employable population.

The considerations of sufficient and insufficient quantitative growth are first made with their respective effects on the real economy. In the real economy, consumer goods and capital goods together with money serve to supply the population.

The real economy is threatened by unemployment, market saturation, shortage of raw materials, shortage of energy, shortage of the environment, partial independence of money in speculative financial markets and lack of money.

The partial independence of money can occur when existing money is no longer needed to maintain real economic cycles. The temptation then arises to speculate with money that is not needed in the real economy and thus to try to earn additional money.

The lack of money in the real economy can be caused by the fact that there are too many people who have too little money to guarantee their livelihood.

In parallel, there are often people who have so much money that they can speculate with part of their income. Other people lack the money for an adequate living. This disparity between the incomes of different groups of people can be caused and exacerbated by asymmetric distribution of income. A special form of asymmetry is the percentage distribution.

One part of the population thus receives larger supplements in the distribution of growth successes and another receives smaller supplements.

Thus, polarization can develop between different population groups. From a global point of view, hungry, very poor and poor groups emerge on the one hand and sufficiently supplied, rich or even super-rich groups on the other hand. Accordingly, they have different amounts of money at their disposal to participate in the real economy. So, on the one hand, there are groups that have too little money available for their livelihood. On the other hand, there are groups of people who do not use a certain amount of their money to purchase goods but use it for purely speculative purposes.

The more polarization between groups of people progresses, the greater are the dangers of discontent, social unrest and ungovernability, triggered by people who have too little money to be able to buy enough goods for survival and for a certain comfort.

Against this background, considerations will be made later on how a self-destructive development driven by polarization could be corrected or at least mitigated.

- Democracy and community tasks
In a democratic state, one of the purposes of elections is to approve proposed solutions to tasks serving the realization of the common good, because such tasks cannot be well accomplished by individuals. These tasks are called community tasks. They include, for example, the social balance among the population as well as internal and external security.

For the realization of the community tasks, the democratic state needs money.

This must be provided by the real economy and thus by the people employed in the real economy, who are also the bearers of democracy.

Democratic election results should be implemented to the greatest possible extent. Majority interests on the one hand and minority interests on the other must be considered. Democratic processes should be as transparent as possible to strengthen the trust in the state.

- Real economy, competition, and secrecy

Demands and offers represent the interests and activities of parties involved in the real economy, as for example: employees, companies, consumers, and investors.

Real economy is essentially characterized by competition. It concerns competition in selling and buying goods. Competitive behavior of the participants is a driving force to achieve competitive advantages. These are realized by people trying to earn and buy more than other people, or to sell more than other people and make a profit.

To achieve advantages in the market over competitors, secrecy is practiced frequently. For example, workers are often not supposed to know each other's earnings This can prevent people with low incomes from feeling dissatisfied or ashamed. Companies keep their market strategy and product planning secret to be able to exploit possible advantages only for themselves and thus build foundations for further business activities. Owners of assets can keep the extent of their assets secret to prevent discussions about envy.

Competitive advantages achieved through secrecy can lay the foundation for further real economic activities, which in the contest with other companies can possibly bring forth new quantitative real economic growth and thus perhaps at least partially stimulate the growth economy.

At first sight, it seems obvious that competitive advantages of some people may possibly come at the expense of others. However, if in a real economic growth episode, a large amount of growth gains is available for distribution, it stands to reason that almost all people in a society can realize growth gains and thus be adequately provided for. Such a situation is characterized by a sufficient increase in the flow of goods and the corresponding flow of money on the buyer and supplier side.

But what happens if the growth gains decrease and thus the possibility to satisfactorily supply the participant with goods is reduced or if a lack of growth gains is a permanent condition? These phenomena will be examined later, particularly from the point of view of a weakening real economy, its causes and how to combat them.

- Quantitative real economic growth and community tasks
People logically seek to obtain goods and money beyond what is necessary for survival. They may then enjoy comfort, acquire status symbols, or consider the future as well secured. The drive for obtaining money and goods is often the competition in which businesses, consumers, investors, and lenders such as banks are involved. Such a drive can generate quantitative real economic growth. In this way, actors in the real economy can profit from growth gains.

However, there are also people who, as disabled people, cannot participate sufficiently in the competitive real economy because of physical or mental disadvantages. It makes sense for the democratically legitimized state to make compensatory payments for these people as part of its community responsibilities. Community tasks also include internal and external security, infrastructure, education, and so on.

The state takes the money required to carry out the common tasks from the pot of growth generated by the real economic actors. This is a redistribution from the real economy to the state. The redistributed money requires little sacrifice from those who generated it, if their growth gains are acceptably greater than the extent of the redistribution.

In return for the redistribution, the society members receive the benefits of a stable state, which is underpinned by performing community tasks. Another pillar of a state's stability is democratic participation. Thus, in democratic elections, the people can participate in determining the common tasks of the state and, on this

30

basis, provide it with the money for the work to be done. They are thus participants in the setting of the community tasks and benefit from the community tasks completed and from the resulting individual satisfaction.

At this point, a dilemma may be mentioned. The members of a democratically organized state are at the same time participants in the associated real economy.

The state, for the purpose of redistribution, takes money from the pool of growth gains However, it should not exhaust this pool, so that sufficient growth benefits remain available to the real economic actors.

The members of the democratic state should also not overuse the pool of money taken by the state for the purpose of redistribution, because if they do, public debts will arise, burdening the future.

Members of the real economy like increasing their advantages. Once these people as members of the democratically organized state also demonstrate real economic behavior in relation to this state, the resulting catalog of state tasks can soon exceed the growth gains provided by the real economy and overburden the state.

- Economy of growth - building bridges between real economy, democracy, and stable state

Apart from the handicapped and disadvantaged people, almost all people can directly participate in growing incomes, profits, and goods within the framework of a sufficiently growing real economy. If this participation increases enough and continuously, there are plenty of reasons to be satisfied with the democratically legitimized state supported by this growth. This assumes that the state fulfills its social tasks, like compensation payments for disabled and disadvantaged people, the ensuring of education, internal and external security etc. It is this constellation within the framework of an economy of growth that obviously builds the bridge between the real economy and democracy as a prerequisite for a stable state.

-    Lack of growth gains and resource reserves
What happens if the expectations of the society members regarding the receipt of growth gains, such as income and profits, supply of goods and security of resources are not adequately fulfilled and possibly cause social dissatisfaction and disputes over distribution? At this point, it may be necessary to consider how such situations can be prevented

Real economic growth is often proposed as a solution to supply problems, to satisfy the people involved by means of growth successes to be achieved and distributed. However, the often-applied asymmetric distribution of growth gains drives polarization above a certain level, which promotes social dissatisfaction.

Apart from ensuring growth gains, the second important issue is the security of resource supply. This might, at first glance, be improved if, in the context of asymmetric distribution of growth gains, the wealth of a few people and the poverty of a lot of people increase. In this way, the increase in resource consumption could be limited, because many poor people would hardly be able to consume resources. For rich people, resources such as in particular the environment available for consumption would thus be available for longer. This ecological polarization, however, would be strengthened in this way.

In this context, it seems sensible to keep the different variants of polarization at appropriately low levels.

First, to this end, the asymmetric distribution of growth successes must move more toward equal distribution to reduce societal and global polarization. This would increase resource consumption.

In the logic of this idea, resource consumption must be limited by sustainable management. Sustainability concerns the use of renewable energies, the recycling of raw materials and the significant reduction of environmental consumption. In this way, the ecological polarization could and should be kept small.

A 4   Overview - From ideals to impact against consequences of polarization

In this field, the following aspects will be discussed:
- ideals
- money and justice
- quantitative real economic growth and the realization of one kind justice
- societal polarization
- ecological polarization
- societal and ecological polarization
- scapegoats
- influence against consequences of polarization with the help of decentralized information technology

- Ideals

Many people have ideals:
They are often in favor of life not being dominated by money.
They wish for a coexistence that is oriented towards justice.
They think it is terrible that people starve, die from hunger or from diseases that are easy to fight, and they want to see this changed.
They find it terrible that too much of resources and especially too much of the environment is consumed and would like that not to happen.

The sum of many ideals can obviously not prevent that parallel to individual ideal states of the world a different kind of real world appears, created by the totality of people.

The real world is characterized by polarization between rich and poor or abundance and hunger. Furthermore, there is the polarization which arises between the times of still sufficient resource supplies and resource shortage. This polarization concerns the environment in particular.

In the following, we will first examine the mechanisms that give rise to and promote polarization. We then consider how the consequences of polarization can be mitigated before they lead to existentially threatening social tensions within and between countries.

On the one hand, polarization gives birth to beneficiaries with sometimes extreme advantages and, on the other hand, ultimately to those who are existentially disadvantaged. This development is to be illuminated and the transparency between the participants is to be improved. Perhaps thereby polarization reduction is possible. Against this background, the real economy, which is a fertile ground for polarization, is divided into five parts

-- The real economy should enable the supply of goods to people.
-- The real economy-oriented financial sector can bring flexibility to the real economy by providing money. This is done in real economic cycles, which ideally consist of goods and money.
-- The speculation-oriented financial economy can develop its own life in the financial economy if the latter opens itself up to pure speculation in addition to real-economy-oriented processes. Pure speculation is an attempt to earn additional money using money without accompanying elements of the real economy.
-- The information economy may take over some of the information tasks of the financial economy within the framework of the real economy. This could be the case if the financial economy partially loses its informational functionality for the real economy under the influence of speculation.
-- In an information-oriented real economy, the secrecy-based drive of the competitive society in the direction of a heavily speculation-based polarization could eased somewhat and readjusted with the help of information technology on a democratic basis.

Polarization may be generated if the real economy reaches its growth limits. This is caused, for example, if money available for distribution is distributed asymmetrically. Thus, some people receive too little money for consumption and hence for the demand for goods. On the other hand, other people receive so much money that they withdraw money from real economic cycles by saving and thus weaken the potential demand for goods The money saved for investments in the real economy is then needed for precisely these purposes in smaller amounts when growth in the real economy also weakens in the light of weakening demand.

Money saved and no longer needed for investment purposes can be used for speculative purposes instead of investment. This may be used to take advantage of opportunities to achieve exchange rate gains through speculation and thus to get additional money.

Bursting speculation bubbles can be a reason to think about alternatives for information, information which is assigned to money, and which is supposed to smooth the real economy. The information economy may be able to offer such alternatives.

The information economy is partly characterized by secrecy. In this case, information is kept secret to perceive competitive advantages.

Thus, secrecy is a driver for a competitive real economy. More comprehensively, it also supports social, global, and environmental polarization.

On the other hand, information technology may also combine the interests of people who are disadvantaged by polarization. Their activities could somewhat loosen secrecy as a driver for polarization on a democratic basis.

- Money and justice

It may seem that the achievement of justice is more oriented to the acquisition of money than to the exchange of mutual gratuitous aid.

For many people, the benchmark for achieving their ideas of justice is probably more determined by claiming to own as much money as other people do. Satisfying such demands seems to be closer to them than first granting money available for distribution to others who have less than they do.

If people considered it primarily fair to distribute available money first to people who own or receive less than they do, then they would have to orient themselves to the lower levels of property of other people. They should not want to adjust their own level to the higher level of other people, but to raise the lower level of other people.

The achievement of the desired justice in the distribution of the available money is obviously primarily oriented towards the higher levels of other people. It is not primarily oriented towards closing the gap between their own higher level and the level of poorer people by raising the lower levels.

The actions taken to achieve equity may initially mean that poorer people also receive more money. Over time, this could lead to a divergence between rich and poor people. This especially happens in combination with asymmetric distribution of the available money. People with higher incomes thus receive a higher supplement than people with lower incomes.

The achievement of desired equity in the distribution of available money tends to be oriented to the higher level of other people rather than to the lower level of other people.

- Quantitative real economic growth and the realization of one kind justice

In the distribution of available money, higher income earners may be a reason why lower income earners also demand more money to be able to afford more goods. The achievement of higher incomes may be made possible by the enhancement of skills.

This logic is seen as a driver of increasing quantitative real economic growth. Many participants thus fulfill their desires by acquiring desired goods and the money required for them. Almost all participants can participate in the distribution of growth successes, which occurs if the demand for goods, labor, and money increases with a tendency towards scarcity. All participants can then demand and receive more step by step.

In this way, needs can be satisfied which, despite popular criticisms of consumerism, become apparent where people buy goods as soon as they are offered, and the money to buy them is available or can be earned

The possibility to receive goods is obviously considered a variation of justice, if almost everyone can participate in the distribution of growth gains, even if some receive more than others.

- Societal polarization

In the case of proportional increases in income, higher incomes receive a larger supplement than lower incomes. Thus, incomes can diverge. If the gap does not become too large, this is obviously acceptable. A gap that is not too large even serves as an incentive not to lose touch with higher incomes to be able to afford more. These correlations illustrate a principle of real economic growth.

However, the differentiation of incomes driven by percentage increases in income does not only serve as an incentive for real economic growth. It is also a driver of social polarization when incomes diverge so much that some people receive so little that their existence is threatened.

Furthermore, social polarization can be additionally driven by automation and rationalization, as will be shown below.

Automation is technology-based. It reduces heavy, one-sided, and monotonous work for people, and it offers recurrence accuracy and routinization advantages. This already indicates the transition to rationalization, which is guided by financial interests. The money invested should be as profitable as possible. The alignment of automation and rationalization suggests that the financial interests in rationalization increasingly dominate the technology-based interests in automation.

On the one hand, automation leads to the improvement of working conditions, facilitation of work and invention of devices that make life more comfortable. On the other hand, especially in combination with rationalization, automation partially causes unemployment, lowers incomes and social polarization, as will be shown below.

The first effect of automation and rationalization is that people are replaced by machinery. However, certain of these people are subsequently needed to produce machinery and information technology, which is used for further automation and rationalization.

Once a certain point in this development has been reached, automation and rationalization will increase productivity in the production of consumer and capital goods to such an extent that a proportion of the human workforce becomes redundant. This is achieved by using energy, machines, robots, and information technology as human amplification factors.

Some people then become unemployed or earn less money in the developing unemployment, e.g., in service industries. The incomes of these people gradually decline, and so does their purchasing power.

Other people will continuously be needed for automation and rationalization if they are trained appropriately. They even tend to receive increasing incomes and can save money and invest it in automation and rationalization. If, with increasing productivity, there is an overabundance of goods and if savings are no longer needed to a sufficient extent for automation and rationalization, then wealthy people will withdraw their money from the real economic cycles by saving it. In this way, potential purchasing power is weakened.

A drive for social polarization is evident. The incomes of one group tend to decrease, those of the other tend to increase. Income reduction of one group and savings of the other group weaken the purchasing power and a quantitative real economic growth.

The preceding discussion shows that asymmetrical increases in income, along with automation and rationalization, can have a polarizing effect on income and potentially weaken purchasing power.

In a polarizing real economy, a reduced proportional share of increasing incomes could logically allow for more equal distribution of income growth gains.

People with low incomes would receive a higher supplement in case of more equal distribution than in case of pure proportional distribution of growth gains They would be able to pursue unsatisfied consumption needs, increase the demand for goods and thus push real economic cycles.

Compared to people with low incomes, people with high incomes would receive lower supplements if income increases were distributed equally than if income increases were distributed on a proportional basis. They would have less money to save, to invest in rationalization, to generate unemployment, and to cause insufficient income increases for low-income people. They would have less money to drive social polarization.

A higher share of equally distributed rather than proportionally distributed income increases would mean an increase in the consumptive share of the real economy as well as a smaller increase in social polarization. There would be no slowdown in the real economy, but an increase in real economic growth gains. Poorer people could benefit from this because they could consume more. In the longer term, more money saved would then be needed again for investment to meet the rising demand for consumer goods.

The increase of equally distributed and the decrease of proportionally distributed shares of the money available for distribution could obviously serve to influence a weakening real economy and an increasing speculative financial economy by saving in the direction of a growing real economy - at the expense of the speculative financial economy.

The reality, however, is that the percentage increase of incomes is based on a social expression of will, which is the sum of many individual behavior patterns. This expression of will is shown by the fact that, despite observable social polarization, there is hardly any equal distribution of income increases Herein, an attempt is made to make this phenomenon plausible.

People who benefit from social polarization find it tempting to classify equal distribution as egalitarianism, and then shape income increases as usual in their own favor. This behavior seems to be made easier, if many people succeed in belonging to the beneficiaries of the proportional distribution of available money and, in parallel, in avoiding the consequences of social polarization.

Proportional increases in income as well as automation and rationalization promote polarization. It takes place between people and population groups. Polarization develops insidiously Its explosive power will be the subject of further considerations.

-      Ecological polarization
The following activities increase consumption and shortage of available resources such as energy, raw materials, and environment:
-      Increase of the human amplification factor
-      Automation and rationalization
-      Equal distribution of growth gains.

These activities can lead supposedly unlimited resource reserves into a state of scarcity. The transition is ecological polarization driven by resource consumption. With it, access to resources develops differently over time for the people involved. The richer people and the richer states have more money to pay for needed resources. Ultimately, however, all people are existentially affected by the consumption of the environment. Ecological polarization will also be the subject of further consideration at a later stage.

-      Societal and ecological polarization
Both variants of polarization can provoke discontent among disadvantaged people This can lead to problems with the acceptance of the state, to social unrest, and distributional conflicts.

The riots resulting from polarization can give rise to social movements which seek social stability in a more authoritarian and less democratic way.

However, the consequences of polarization could also be prevented, e.g., by appropriately skimming off gains on speculative financial markets in particular to redistribute them to poorer parts of the population and countries.

On the other hand, resistance from those who profit from polarization is to be expected, because these people also profit from the fact that poor people receive as little money as possible for consumption and thus reduce the resource reserve as little as possible. Thus, resource reserves last longer for those with large financial potentials.

There are logically limits to the acceptance of polarization on the part of the disadvantaged

Those limits may awaken the interest of the beneficiaries of polarization in finding scapegoats, to hold responsible for the emergence of polarization.

- Scapegoats
First, it is necessary to elucidate the principle of finding scapegoats. In a first step, we consider the interaction of disadvantaged people from different countries. On the one hand, there are refugees from famine or war zones who have fled to industrialized countries. On the other hand, there are poor people in industrialized countries. In a first approach it seems obvious to hold refugees responsible for the fact that there are poor people in their countries of refuge, because the refugees get money and jobs at the expense of the poor local people. It is often ignored that the disadvantage of people in industrialized countries is often caused by social polarization in the industrialized countries themselves, and that refugees from hunger and war zones are often the result of global polarization between rich and poor countries.

People bearing the negative consequences of social and global polarization are obviously all in it together These are poor people in impoverished states and poor people in industrialized states. These people are strangers to each other, which can be used politically to play them off against each other. Insofar, refugees are held up as scapegoats for fundamental problems of polarization Thus, further considerations are necessary.

- Counteracting the effects of polarization using decentralized information technology

For those disadvantaged by polarization, it is logical that they may want to acquire goods in increasing quantities. Finally, many people also want to obtain more goods. To satisfy the demand for goods, the production of goods is necessary. To enable increasing production, people equip themselves with amplification factors by using energy, machines, automats, and information technology. With their help, automation becomes possible, and this is combined with the interest in rationalization for the purpose of profitable use of money. This improves productivity in the production of consumer and capital goods Thus, more and more resources - like energy, raw materials and especially the limited environment - are consumed, so that their shortage becomes imminent.

This way of thinking shows a vicious circle. In the end, covering the increasing need for goods for everyone brings about a resource shortage which then limits the realization of product demand. In the following we consider the possibility of escaping from this vicious circle.

In an ideal situation, markets would be able to meet the demand for goods and at the same time prevent resource shortages. However, markets are apparently designed for growth with the associated scarcity of resources. This is because people increasingly demand more goods for survival and consumption and for improved living standards without sufficient consideration of resource reserves.

Primarily, it makes sense to deal with real economic growth, which serves to cover the peoples need for goods. For this purpose, we will consider two forms of growth.

First, a sufficient quantitative growth of the real economy is of importance. In this context, human labor, automation, and rationalization increasingly stimulate real economic cycles. These consist of resources to produce goods, goods, wages, salaries, consumption, profit, and investment. If almost all members of a society are well equipped with money and goods and if their wishes for survival, comfort, status symbols and future security are largely fulfilled, there is sufficient quantitative real economic growth.

Secondly, sufficient quantitative growth in the real economy can turn into insufficient quantitative growth in the real economy. This happens, for example, because of the interaction of automation and rationalization with the asymmetric distribution of growth gains. A special form of asymmetry is the percentage increase of wages and salaries.

Automation and rationalization increase the growth gains. If these are distributed asymmetrically and, in a special case, on a percentage basis, one part of the population receives larger supplements and another part smaller ones. Here is a gap in the amount of income of the people involved. For people with low incomes, there are fewer consumption opportunities. At the same time, automation and rationalization increase productivity and the output of goods. Decreasing consumption possibilities and more productive output of goods will require less labor This results in a lower demand for labor and lower incomes.

We have seen how asymmetric distribution of growth gains leads to a divergence in the income of the people involved. Of course, this also applies to a special case of asymmetry, namely the proportional increase in wages and salaries, which makes some employees relatively poorer. On the other hand, the people needed for automation and rationalization receive higher supplements to their incomes. They become relatively richer. As a result of this split, people with higher incomes withdraw part of the growth gains from consumption by saving, while other people can only develop less purchasing power because their incomes are too low. Both groups weaken the real economy.

For an increasing part of the population, the divergence of incomes offers hardly any opportunities to move up the income scale. Such a rise in relative poverty of population groups can cause social and global discontent.

When discussing this phenomenon of the partial impoverishment of a society, people often propose traditional quantitative growth in the real economy as an instrument for solving the problem. This is supposed to produce growth gains that can be distributed. However, it is contradictory to almost universally utilize quantitative real-economic growth to combat partial poverty, since it is often shown to be the very cause of it. Nevertheless, the economic discussion primarily relies on the instrument of real economic growth because of an apparent lack of alternatives.

If growth gains were distributed asymmetrically or in percentages only to a lesser extent and distributed equally to a greater extent, there would be less polarization between rich and poor people or between people living in hunger and those living in abundance. We have seen how asymmetric distribution of growth gains leads to a divergence in the income of the people involved. This would then allow more and more consumer and investment goods to be purchased However, this could then also lead to increasingly rapid shortage of resources.

If growth gains are distributed asymmetrically to the maximum extent possible, there will be poor and hungry people to the maximal possible extent and rich and abundant people to the minimal possible extent. In these contexts, the shortage of resources would proceed rather slowly.

The following tension between more equal and more asymmetric distribution of growth gains emerges:

If growth gains are distributed more equally, real economic growth will be driven and the scarcity of resources in terms of energy, raw materials and especially the environment will be intensified. Logically, against such a development, the beneficiaries of the asymmetric distribution of growth gains will feel called upon to secure resource stocks for themselves for a longer period through asymmetric distribution.

The asymmetric distribution of growth gains drives the social polarization between the disadvantaged and the beneficiaries. Such a development can provoke the disadvantaged to demonstrate and exert influence.

Against this background, societal, global, and ecological polarization must be considered in relation to real economic growth and resource shortage to identify possibilities to reduce societal disruption.

In a first step, we consider the stabilization of real economic growth for the purpose of providing sufficient growth gains for all members of society.

In a second step, we integrate the limited availability of resources into our consideration, particularly those of the consumable environment.

In the next step, information technology could play a role in overcoming the consequences of social, global, and ecological polarization. This may be done by using it to reduce secrecy in the competitive society, if secrecy acts as a driver of social, global, and ecological polarization. For this purpose, decentralized disadvantaged individual interests could unite, plan anti-secrecy measures based on information technology, and implement them on a democratic basis.

Further, we consider the real economic development including special social aspects.

After this overview, we will first discuss basic considerations of goods, money, and exchange relations.

B   Goods, money and exchange relationships

Whatever people GIVE, TAKE or even STORE INTERMEDI-ATELY is summarized under the collective term goods. These include, for example, attention, affection, communication, voluntary assistance, food, services, consumer goods, capital goods, raw materials and energy. This enumeration also includes financial resources such as money. They can serve as means of exchange for many other goods.

The range of all goods can be divided into three categories:
- financial resources
- qualitative goods
- quantitative goods.

By giving and taking goods, people enter relationships, respectively - exchange relationships.

Even an existence as a hermit is included in this definition due to its interaction with nature and its goods in the form of its resources.

Qualitative and quantitative goods as well as financial resources can be exchanged. Therefore, the entirety of human cooperation can be pictured this way.

B 1   Financial resources and exchange relationships

Financial resources can serve as a general means of exchange for a broad variety of other goods.

Money is a form of financial means. It is assigned a value expressed in the form of a number and a currency.

Money is needed to buy or sell goods. When not used, it can be stored, saved, lent or borrowed. It is used, among other things, to form real economic cycles in combination with goods.

- Intermediate storage

Money can be easily stored in the periods between exchanges. Then, it is not necessary to store goods that take up space or are perishable in order to exchange them later for other goods that take up space or are perishable.

- Saving

You can save money to make larger purchases later on.

- Borrowing and lending

You can also borrow money from other people or institutions or lend it to them. This money can be used, for example, to bring forward investments and take advantage of market opportunities as early as possible. With its help, however, it is also possible to realize consumption opportunities ahead of time.

B 2 Qualitative goods and exchange relationships

Qualitative goods are defined here in a way that no monetary value is assigned to them. To improve transparency, their meaning is defined as follows:
- Forms of appearance of qualitative goods
- Qualitative goods and the time required for developing trust and exchange relationships.
- Qualitative goods and the time required for their acquisition, which depends on the complexity of the exchange market and the time required for the intermediate storage of good.

- Forms of appearance of qualitative goods

-- Qualitative goods exist among other things as immaterial goods.
These are, for instance, goods such as attention and care, listening and communication - goods that people need as a social being, but which are mostly not acquired or given in exchange for money.

-- Qualitative goods also appear as unpaid help.
Qualitative goods also include unpaid help. They are e.g. given to friends, neighbors, relatives, members of a group or people in need of help. Often this is mutual help.

-- Quantitative goods get a qualitative character, if there is a shortage of money.
If many people in a real economy have too little money to buy all the goods or services they need, alternatives arise. These people then produce food for their own needs, and also produce a surplus which they use as a means of exchange to acquire other food. Exchanged goods from the surplus thus acquire a qualitative character.

This suggests that goods and money should be approximately in a balance and characterized by relative scarcity in order to enable incentives for real economic cycles of goods and money.

If too little money flows into poor countries because other, rich countries pay too little money for raw materials and product manufacturing, hardly any real economic cycles can develop in the poor countries with too little money. The economy of scarcity does not allow many people in poor countries to acquire many goods and consume many raw materials. Thus, rich countries profit as long as possible from global raw materials and the poverty they in turn reinforce.

-- Quantitative goods get a qualitative character if there is too much money in circulation and money ownership loses value too quickly.

Goods that market participant [1] could acquire for money from market participant [2] are not willingly given away for money by [2] if the money accepted by [2] loses too much value with him until the next use.

The loss of the value of money may occur during the period of intermediate storage from collection to spending due to inflation. Inflation, in turn, can be caused by the fact that too much money is put into circulation without a corresponding equivalent value of desired goods being available for purchase. Then it is evident for suppliers of goods to increase the prices of their goods. Thus, the money in circulation and the prices of goods can increase rapidly. However, the money stored temporarily by consumers and companies does not increase and later only permits the purchase of goods that have become less expensive in the meantime.

If such a development takes on considerable proportions, foreign goods may no longer be acquired for money but by exchanging them for one's own goods. In addition, exchange objects for later required goods may be procured. The objects of exchange are thus temporarily stored until the next exchange and thus deprived of the real economic supply of the population for a certain time. The original scarcity of goods is thus additionally increased. The goods that can otherwise be bought take on the character of qualitative goods.

This fact suggests that goods and money should remain approximately in balance and be marked by relative shortage in order to facilitate the functioning of real-economic cycles.

-- Quantitative goods take on a qualitative character when there are causally not enough goods available.

In a centrally planned economy as a special form of an economy, experience shows that there are often too few goods available for purchase. The members of this society could have enough money to fulfill their wishes, if there were enough goods available in all areas. If there are not enough goods offered for the money available in some areas, desired goods often cannot be purchased. If the suppliers of goods notice the shortage, it is likely that they want to increase the prices of the goods when money is abundant, because they could still sell the goods. However, when prices are fixed in a planned economy and may not be raised in a prevailing market situation, it is obvious that the suppliers of goods will not offer their goods in exchange for money if there is an alternative. This alternative often is that goods suppliers exchange their goods for other goods and these received goods in return exchange for other goods needed by themselves. Thus, goods on the exchange market may achieve a higher perceived exchange value than if they were sold for money.

Goods that are actually offered for money thus acquire the character of qualitative goods as exchange goods. If exchange of goods prevails, it indicates that the function of money has failed. This fact, as well, suggests that goods and money should remain approximately in balance and be characterized by relative shortage to enable the function of real-economic cycles.

- Qualitative goods and the time required for developing trust and exchange relationships.
The value of qualitative goods is often not easily measurable. Giving and taking often cannot be well balanced. Furthermore, if giving and taking occurs at different times, the parties must be sure that one side will not break off the exchange relationship at a time of imbalance to their benefit. Exchange partners should trust each other in such a way that there can and will be a mutually perceived balance between giving and taking over a longer period of time.
It therefore seems reasonable to assume that it takes a while to build up trust between exchange partners, whereas goods can be acquired more quickly with money. The time required to build trust

is likely to be longer the greater the perceived value of exchange objects.

Trust-building is important for the emergence and long-term existence of exchange relations.

- Qualitative goods and the time required for their acquisition, which depends on the complexity of the exchange market and the time required for the intermediate storage of goods.
When there is not enough money or goods available or if money is not accepted for its lack of stable value, goods are purchased through the exchange of goods instead. The exchange relations between a multitude of people in interaction with a large number of goods are then very complex. Thereby, the communicative and cooperative skills of the participants are challenged in order to realize the distribution of goods on the market.

Since goods are often stored temporarily in exchange relations, sometimes for longer periods, they are temporarily removed from consumption and, in some cases, from investment activities. This impedes the provision of goods to the population.

Finding and acquiring the desired goods through exchange often takes more time than acquiring goods directly in exchange for money given the complexity of the exchange process and the time needed for temporary storage.

B 3 Quantitative goods and exchange relationships

Quantitative goods are those to which a monetary value has been assigned. They include, for example, raw materials energy, capital goods, consumer goods and services. Acquiring quantitative goods with money is usually faster than acquiring qualitative goods by exchanging them for other qualitative goods.

B 4 The interaction of quantitative and qualitative goods

Qualitative and quantitative goods show different lengths of time required for acquiring either qualitative or quantitative goods. These time spans are called asymmetric times.

Furthermore, the shares of qualitative and quantitative goods in the quantity of all exchanged goods influence each other.

- The asymmetry of the amount of time required for the acquisition of qualitative or quantitative goods

The time required to establish a relationship of trust between exchange partners, the complexity of the exchange market and the associated intermediate storage time for qualitative goods make it obviously more time-consuming to realize exchanges involving qualitative goods than to acquire quantitative goods with the help of money. We may speak of an asymmetry of the times embodied in the acquisition of qualitative goods on the one hand and quantitative goods on the other hand. Thus, a goods market with qualitative goods works explicably slower than a comparable market with quantitative goods.

- Quantitative goods and their decreasing trade share in favor of qualitative goods

If the share of money and the share of goods in real economic cycles are not in an appropriate ratio, people often exchange quantitative goods for other quantitative goods in addition to the typical qualitative goods, without using money as a medium of exchange. Quantitative goods exchanged for each other thus acquire the character of qualitative goods. The share of qualitative goods in the total volume of goods exchanged thus tends to increase.

- Quantitative goods and their increasing trade share at the expense of qualitative goods

A disadvantage of exchanging qualitative goods is that the exchange partners may unilaterally break off relations after receiving goods perceived as valuable and break down mutual trust.

Thus, qualitative exchange relationships might not exist permanently. This is especially true if people have enough money at their disposal, if enough goods are offered and if money is trusted as a stable medium of exchange. Then it seems plausible that people increasingly rely on quantitative goods and that their share of the total goods market increases.

B 5   Summary: Goods and exchange relationships

It is assumed as reasonable that the interaction of people can be described by representing their exchange relations - including the use of money.

People can acquire qualitative goods by exchanging qualitative goods. Thus, they can try to acquire everything that should not or cannot be bought for money. Thereby people learn to understand each other. They are supposed to be able to communicate, to negotiate and to act. Acquiring qualitative goods can even be seen as a drive to gain socio-psychological competencies. Exchange transactions with qualitative goods can be described as a lubricant for social interaction.

People can acquire quantitative goods using money. They may earn the money required for this, for example, by working to produce goods.

Goods basically exist to enable people to fulfill needs and meet demands. People can also show how much they can afford. Generally, we can say that most people have desires and try to fulfill them.

The creation of desires often happens more quickly and easily than the act of earning and acquiring the desired goods. First of all, it can be assumed that desires do not dry up and can thus continue to act as an impetus for quantitative real economic growth.

The desires for goods, the human work to be done for their fulfillment and the production process of the goods are central real economic elements. Real economic growth is shown by the increase in the production of goods. Along with money already available or to be acquired, this production of goods forms real economic cycles. Thus, a driver of quantitative real economic growth can emerge.

C   Drivers of the quantitative real economy

Experience shows that people want to fulfill their wishes continuously and to an increasing extent. The real economy can be used to provide desired goods. First and foremost, these are quantitative goods, because they can be used to fulfill desires quickly through the purchase process, provided that the necessary money is available or can be acquired. In this context, a quantitative real economy characterized by growth can emerge. In the following, we will break this down in order to look at its drivers.

-        Quantitative growth in the real economy and its enhancement by increasing productivity

When the quantity of goods and the income in real economic cycles increase continuously, we refer to this as quantitative real economic growth. Companies then produce more and more goods and employ more and more workers for this purpose, who in turn earn more and more money for the acquisition of further quantitative goods. In this process, companies can realize profits and invest in increasing productivity. Productivity increases are made possible by the use of raw materials, machinery, information technology and external energy. Here, a strengthening real economic cycle was shown, whereby the increase of the produced goods and provided incomes is made possible primarily by the increase of productivity. The gains specifically in wages and salaries are referred to as growth gains.

Income of employees in particular, profits of enterprises, production of goods and acquisition of goods are continuously leveling off against each other in the described processes. This leveling should be done in small steps for almost all participants. The success of increasing productivity should be passed on to employees and companies. The increase then offers an improvement for all parties involved, so that they logically have an interest in continuing the development within the framework of quantitative real economic growth.

2024-05-26

- Quantitative real economic growth and scarcity

Quantitative real economic growth can be triggered and maintained in two ways.

First, with demand for goods and increasing production of goods, labor and labor time can become scarce. Thus, higher incomes are enforceable and the opportunities to purchase goods increase.

Second, as demand for goods increases and there is a potential shortage of goods, which may be reflected in longer delivery times, companies can achieve good prices. If this results in good profits, they can use these to invest in new and more efficient production facilities and in higher incomes for employees, among other things.

Both types of drive are based on scarcity. This is, first, the scarcity of labor and, second, the potential scarcity of available goods. Impending scarcity of goods can be compensated by an increase in the production of goods, which in turn causes scarcity of labor. This can be compensated using machinery, which in turn requires more labor for its production.

- Cycles of the real economy

In the real economy, we are dealing with cycles. These can be primarily of a real economic nature or primarily of a speculative financial nature. Speculative-financial cycles will be discussed later.

The figure at the end of the book shows an example of a real economic cycle as part of an economic network. At the beginning of the cycle (from 1 to 2) is the "labor for the production of quantitative goods". The goods then move on (from 3 to 4) to the "acquisition of quantitative goods". In the opposite direction, money flows to pay for the goods (from 5 to 6) and for the labor (from 7 to 8). In this way, a real economic cycle is described. It is a symbolic cycle. In one direction, goods are produced and purchased, and in the opposite direction, the corresponding payments are made.

Using this model, it is clear that goods flow from production to acquisition in one direction, are then consumed, and logically must be continuously replaced by new ones. Since resources such as energy, raw materials and the environment are used to produce the goods, it can already be seen here that resource consumption and resource scarcity are increasingly programmed with increasing consumption.

To continuously pay for the flow of goods (from 1 to 4) (from 5 to 8), the money needs a return flow (from 9 to 10). This describes that after the payment of labor (8), the money is in the hands of people who can then use it to pay for further goods (5) via 9 and 10.

The flows of goods and money are connected by transfer points. The transfer points can be seen as warehouses for goods and for money. If the transfer points are almost empty, this indicates that money and goods are constantly in motion and in short supply.

If for the purpose of satisfaction of needs and fulfillment of desires more and more goods are demanded and paid with earned money, quantitative real economic growth is shown. Since the human labor force for the realization of growth quickly reaches its limits, just like the human capacity for information processing, the necessity of machinery, energy and information technology becomes apparent.

-       Real economic cycles create a network
The model shown in the figure at the end of the book includes the production of goods as well as their respective payment. Thus, it is possible to imagine a real economic cycle. Furthermore, there are other real economic cycles. Within these cycles, for example, innovative products and status goods move, mostly in connection with the work for their production. In addition, money flows for the

respective payment. The cycles are interconnected and form a network. The description is given in the figure at the end of the book.

The real economic cycles are considered from the point of view of how they are driven and how this can cause quantitative real economic growth.

-      Real economic drivers
There are obvious human desires for securing survival, acquiring comfort and acquiring status symbols, or securing the future for oneself and for children. These initially hardly limited desires cause an increasing demand for quantitative goods. To produce these goods, more and more labor force is needed. The increasing earnings of these workers generate more and more purchasing power, which in turn enables them to buy more and more goods.

Quantitative goods and labor income are thus real economic drivers with the help of which human desires can be fulfilled. Against the background of scarcely dwindling desires, quantitative real economic growth can thus unfold.

Growth obviously requires further real economic drivers, the most important of which are presented below. The presentation does not claim to be exhaustive. It is merely intended to give an impression of the complexity of real economic activity and the many ways in which quantitative real economic growth can be influenced.

C 1   Central driver of the real economy: Satisfaction of the demand with quantitative goods

Quantitative goods are at the heart of a market economy, to the extent that needs are not already met by qualitative goods. What is necessary is that the money required to meet the demand for quantitative goods is available. This money can be earned, for example, through the labor required to manufacture the products. By paying for the desired goods, real economic cycles are closed.

The real economy thus comes about through the interaction of quantitative goods with money. As a distinction to this, the speculative-oriented financial economy can be described in such a way that it allows attempts to earn additional money only with the help of money, without quantitative goods having to play an essential role. The speculative use of money will be considered later.

It is assumed that desires for quantitative goods lie dormant in almost all people, to be fulfilled according to possibility. Fulfillment of desires serves e.g. to secure survival or to enable comfort and the acquisition of status symbols. Desires, needs and requirements of people are sources and drives for the demand for quantitative goods. They are central drivers of quantitative growth in the real economy.

Meeting the demand for quantitative goods usually takes place together with other drivers such as the workforce. The following observations on various real economic drivers are limited to the period in which certain facts are given. Thus, it is for instance necessary that people can have enough money to purchase quantitative goods, that markets are not saturated and that sufficient resources exist to allow quantitative real economic growth to be realized.

C 2   Direct real economic driver: Human resources

If, in times of rising demand for quantitative goods, the required quantity of human resources increases and, in the course of this development, manpower becomes short, workers can relatively easily push through demands to increase incomes. If these are not met, employers must expect employees to move to other companies. This means that employers will meet requirements that are appropriate to the real economy in order to be able to profitably exploit market opportunities. When employees' income rises, they also have more money available for consumption. Their purchasing power increases and with it the possibility of satisfying the demand for quantitative goods. As long as employees do not save income resulting from an increasing demand for quantitative goods but soon spend it again and buy quantitative goods, quantitative growth in the real economy will increase.

C 3   Direct real economic driver:
Current account surplus

In most cases, quantitative goods are not only produced and consumed in the home country. Exports and imports also take place. If a country's imports and exports do not have the same volume, this results in a current account gap. This can be expressed as a current account surplus or a current account deficit.

To produce the goods which generate the current account surplus, labor force is needed. This generates additional purchasing power in the exporting countries. As soon as this purchasing power leads to increased demand, direct additional quantitative real economic growth becomes possible.

In countries with a current account deficit caused by imports of machinery, this can trigger technological development that helps to reduce future imports. Thus, a current account deficit would only be necessary temporarily.

C 4   Indirect real economic driver: Waste of goods

At the day of the best-before date, the difference between presumed large and realized smaller demand for food is often given away to waste.

The waste can be caused by the production and provision of food on a generous scale in order to be able to maintain a sufficient supply for possible peak demand. In this way, suppliers can demonstrate to consumers that they can purchase all products in desired quantities at any time.

This is perhaps intended to give customers an incentive to drift to the competition, which could happen if a product were not available. But perhaps it is also intended to counter a hidden archaic fear of hunger. But perhaps a surplus of supply is also necessary to give the market economy a security-of-supply label.

The production costs for the destroyed superfluous goods must be additionally generated by the revenues for the sold goods. In this way, a real economic cycle is indirectly closed, because products that are produced but not sold are paid for by the purchase of other goods. On the one hand, this indirectly drives growth in the real economy. On the other hand, the purchasing power used for wasted goods could be used by the paying consumers for other desired goods if the waste of goods were avoided.

C 5 Accompanying real economic driver: Resource consumption

In addition to human labor, the production of quantitative goods requires resources such as raw materials and energy. For the increasing supply, processing and production of resources, labor is needed. Their earnings generate purchasing power and enable the additional acquisition of quantitative goods. As soon as this purchasing power leads to additional consumption, accompanying additional quantitative real economic growth can result.

C 6 Real economic driver at higher supply level: Innovative products

Technical progress is driven, among other things, by human curiosity or by people investing in research and development. As a result, innovative products and product variants can be made available to consumers and producers. The aim is to make offers to people who are happy to accept innovations and the resulting benefits. Innovations enable such people to make their lives more pleasant, easier and more effective. Beyond satisfying basic needs, innovative products and product variants offer the possibility of triggering additional quantitative real economic growth if money is available or becomes available for such products at a higher supply level.

C 7 Real economic drivers at higher supply level: Status symbols and status goods

The acquisition of quantitative goods as status symbols or status goods serves, among other things, to gain status and recognition. This can happen quickly because status symbols and status goods are quickly presentable after purchase.

Status gain and recognition fade quickly when, in the race for status gain and social recognition, competing people have acquired the same goods as the person himself. Then an incentive for a new round of acquiring new status symbols and status goods appears.

Just as addiction can apparently increase an addict's need for addictive drugs on its own, addiction-like sensations also seem to be able to drive the need for status symbols and status goods.

The fulfillment of desire through the acquisition of status symbols and status goods can be interpreted as a drive for quantitative growth of the real economy. This process appears like a perpetuum mobile of the real economy.

To produce goods for status gain and recognition, labor and resources are needed. The earnings of additionally needed workers create new purchasing power. If demand is quickly created, the addictive potential of the buyers of status symbols and status goods generates additional quantitative growth in the real economy. Since desires for status symbols and status goods are dormant in many places, they can generate additional growth as soon as money is released for them in the course of growth after the basic needs have been satisfied.

C 8 Real economic drivers: Environmental protection, use of renewable energy and recycling

Resources such as raw materials, energy and the consumable environment are used to produce quantitative goods. The consumption of such resources causes material waste, losses of used forms of energy and environmental damage during product manufacture. When manufactured products have completed their use cycle, they also become waste. This development can be counteracted through recycling, the use of renewable energy and environmental protection.

- Recycling

Increasing the production of goods leads to an increase in the consumption of raw materials. The accompanying shortage of raw material resources can be reduced by recycling production waste and discarded products.

- Use of renewable energy

The use of renewable energy can reduce the use of environmentally harmful non-renewable energy.

- Environmental protection

Discarded products, production waste and the use of fossil energy often cause environmental pollution. When this increases, it leads to a shortage of environmental resources. This can be partly countered with environmental protection measures.

- Prices fail to regulate consumption

In some cases, it is only profitable to recycle, use renewable energy and protect the environment when too many resources have already been consumed from the perspective of safeguarding the future. As a result, when resources are scarce, price may not act as a consumption regulator until resource supplies have already over-shrunk. This price-related over-consumption of resources can be described as a "wasting" process in regards to their scarcity.

It is evidently the logic of the market that resources are sometimes consumed wastefully until they become too scarce and are lost for future generations. The price as a means of regulating the consumption of resources often proves to be an instrument that is effective too late.

For this reason, the principle of sustainability is forcing its way into considerations of securing supply. This sustainability should help to reduce the use of resources such as raw materials, non-renewable energy and the consumable environment. To conserve resources, it recognizes the means of recycling, the use of renewable energy and environmental protection.

As long as the costs of sustainable resources such as recycled raw materials, renewable energy and protected environment are higher than for resources directly available for consumption such as raw materials, non-renewable energy and unprotected environment, the additional price makes up the subsidies to be paid for the sustainability to be achieved.

Against this background, the market can be described as follows. If Company A recycles to recover resources, uses renewable energy, and provides environmental protection, it may be pushed out of the market by Company B, which uses cheaper directly provided raw materials, cheaper non-renewable energy, and environment ready for consumption without protecting it.

The insufficient use of recycled raw materials and the excessive use of non-renewable energy, as well as the excessive consumption of the environment, are obviously a logical consequence of a real economy in which prices act insufficiently as a regulator of resource supplies. Such a This development poses existential dangers resulting from resource scarcity, especially in terms of the environment.

A discussion is emerging, on the one hand, about a market economy and its potential for self-destruction and, on the other hand, about the obvious need for intervention in order to secure supplies and thus a future through sustainability.

-      Environmental protection and the intervention of the state
A special logic regarding the realization of sustainability can be seen in environmental pollution. This pollution is caused by many individual people and affects all people as an overall result. Environmental protection thus becomes, at least in part, a community

task. It can partly be carried out based on legally defined regulations at the expense of the polluter. In some cases, this common task is carried out directly by the state. As long as the people involved accept the necessities and see the successes, acceptance of these implementations is more likely.

- Sustainability and technical progress

In the areas of recycling, renewable energy and environmental protection, technical progress is often driven by applied sustainability. This may also be reflected in export successes if it brings competitive advantages over other countries. This can lead to growth successes in the exporting countries.

C 9 Real economic driver accompanying growth driver: Investments

Investments are used, among other things, to realize automation and rationalization. This is achieved using machinery, energy and information technology. This often makes workers redundant.

- Automation

Human curiosity seems to be a feasible reason for people to do research and development and to make Inventions. An incentive for targeted automation is probably to facilitate and also replace human labor with machinery, external energy and information technology, ultimately reducing the use of labor for financial reasons.

- Rationalization

Possible savings of human labor through automation and parallel financial exploitation interests generate a drive for rationalization in some people. Automation then serves to be able to perform routine work increasingly more cheaply, quickly and reliably. The

use of rationalization usually requires additional financial resources beyond those for automation, but aiming at increasing
profitability.

- Investments
The purpose of automation and rationalization is, among other
things, to improve the conditions for generating company profits
in order to be able to use realized profits for investments in research, development and production facilities or also to distribute
them to sought-after workers so that they do not switch to other
companies.

On the one hand, automation and rationalization make workers
superfluous; on the other hand, workers are needed for the realization of automation and rationalization. As long as, ultimately,
more people are needed for the realization of automation and rationalization than jobs are lost through it, the conditions for quantitative growth in the real economy will be improved. For this purpose, the extent of the production of goods with the help of automation and rationalization and the resulting purchasing power of
the labor force are considered.

If investments in automation and rationalization do not overfill the
demand for quantitative goods, and thus do not lead to market
saturation and, if in parallel, the purchasing power increases, the
growth of the real economy can rise, insofar as the income and
profits generated are quickly reintegrated into real economic
cycles.

Hence, whether quantitative real economic growth driven by investments in automation and rationalization takes place to a sufficient extent depends on two parallel strands of development.
These are a sufficiently large labor force and its sufficiently increased purchasing power as well as the corresponding values
of manufactured and sold goods.

2024-05-26

C 10 Time-delayed driver of the real economy: Education

To realize technical progress in the form of innovative products, automation and rationalization, it is usually necessary to offer education. The term education covers training, knowledge transfer and science.

Education and technical progress can bring competitive advantages for some enterprises or also countries, if they invest more in education and technical progress than other enterprises and countries do. To promote education, states, companies and also individual members of a society make the expenditures that are considered necessary or affordable.

The promotion of education tends to have a delayed effect on growth because it takes time for the effect of education to show up in the quantitative real economy.

C 11 Balancing real economic drivers: Savings and loans

Real economic cycles consist of, among other things, quantitative goods and money.

Money is suitable for people to save it for themselves. But it can also be lent to other people, institutions or companies. Saved money or loans can be used, for example, to build houses, buy cars, finance the production of goods or make investments in the production of goods. Loans can also be used to bring forward the purchase of consumer goods. Savings and loans can of course also be combined.

The government can try to influence quantitative growth in the real economy through incentives to save or borrow. It can, for example, use the promotion of building savings to calm down excessive quantitative growth in the real economy. However, it can also try to counteract weak growth through low borrowing costs.

C 12   A rather growth-neutral driver of the real economy:
Redistribution to fulfil common tasks of the state

Periods of sufficient quantitative real economic growth are defined by the provision of sufficient growth gains for all stakeholders. The state should also receive money, namely for the fulfilment of community tasks that should primarily be carried out by the state and less by the individual members of society. Community tasks include, for example, care for disabled people, internal and external security and education.

In other words, there should be a satisfactory level of growth for the people involved. If, in parallel, for the purpose of carrying out community tasks, the state diverts an accepted share of the growth benefits for itself, a stable and democratic form of society can emerge for which most of the participants are happy to divert growth benefits.

The diversions in favor of the state have the function of redistribution. In times of sufficient quantitative real economic growth, these tend to have a growth-neutral effect after being used by the state. However, if the growth benefits collected by the state come from people with a high propensity to save and are then quickly spent again by the state in the direction of real economic cycles, additional quantitative real economic growth can result.

It might be important that redistribution towards community tasks is limited in such a way that the growth gains for the individual sector do not bleed out.

Sufficient fulfilment of individual desires for quantitative goods and sufficient fulfilment of community tasks by the state with the help of redistributed money bring social stability as the basis for a democratic state in times of permanent sufficient real economic growth. For this purpose, the members of society have to make hardly noticeable sacrifices as long as, despite redistribution, sufficient quantitative real economic growth is guaranteed and this yields sufficient growth results for all.

C 13 Summary: Quantitative real economy and its growth with the help of real economic drivers

The real economy is a complex entity. In a first step we have distinguished between goods that are not bought for money and those that are bought for money. So-called quantitative goods, which are bought with money, can fulfil people's wishes more quickly than so-called qualitative goods, which have to be bought in exchange for other goods. Thus, quantitative goods are often preferred.

If, after basic needs have been met, people want to live increasingly better, more pleasantly and more comfortably or also want to realize more prestige or bragging rights, the fulfilment of further desires is taken into consideration. To satisfy these desires, quantitative real economic growth seems to be necessary. Real economic drivers come into play to realize growth. Through the interaction of the drivers, the real economy presents itself as a complex structure, as a network, in which many drivers are to keep the supply of society with quantitative real economic goods on an expansion course.

In the phase in which there is sufficient quantitative real economic growth and sufficient growth successes are realized, most individuals can realize many of their individual desires with the help of the growth successes. Thus, there is an overall societal interest in the preservation and stability of this growth-oriented society if, in parallel, community tasks are sufficiently fulfilled by the state, for which it derives growth gains to an acceptable extent.

Growth in the real economy functions like a control loop that is driven and kept running by desires and their fulfilment. The combined continuous and increasing fulfilment of desires of the individual causes quantitative real economic growth. This is generated by the production of quantitative goods, the payment for the work done and the purchase of the goods produced and increases step by step due to further desires. The growth thus generated helps to fulfil the desires of the individuals. The result is a permanently improved supply of quantitative goods for almost all participants. Many different drivers of the real economy interact and form a network, as shown in the figure at the end of the book.

To ensure the depicted development as a combination of sufficient permanent quantitative real economic growth with
- the fulfilment of community tasks by the state
- personal satisfaction of the members of society
- stability of the state
- the democratic society
there is a need for various accompanying considerations made in the next section.

D   The real economy and its players

Quantitative real economic cycles consist of the flow of goods in one direction and the flow of money in the opposite direction.

In each flow there are storage areas. On the one hand, there are storage areas for goods, e.g. between the production of goods and their distribution. On the other hand, there are storage areas for money where saved money can be temporarily stored and from where it can be lent out in the meantime.

There are changes in the cycle of goods and money. Increases are more likely to be targeted. In this way, an increasing population can be satisfied. Furthermore, many people demand an improvement in their supply of goods and money.

The increase in the goods flow and money flow is referred to as quantitative real economic growth. Growth is driven, for example, using machinery, energy, information technology, human labor and money.

In general, real economic cycles, i.e. quantitative as well as qualitative, are characterized by changes. In this context, the following aspects will be discussed:
- Quantitative real economic growth and monetary stability
- Quantitative real economic growth and qualitative growth
- Quantitative real economic growth - stability and democracy
- Exchange relations with qualitative goods - Stability of barter societies

D 1   Quantitative real economic growth and monetary stability

Real economic cycles also include quantitative goods and money People who use money as a means of payment must be able to trust that the value of money remains stable so that money saved does not lose too much of its value during the period of temporary storage. To ensure the stability of the value of money, the following elements should be considered.

People and institutions can get money, e.g. through work, entrepreneurial activity, inheritance, gifts, receipt of pensions or also through transfer payments from the state. With money, people can fulfil their desires by acquiring quantitative good. Since desires easily increase faster than the acquisition of money, it is quite logical that money is often perceived as being short.

If major social groups can acquire a disproportionate amount of money for the purpose of acquiring goods, and they then want to buy much more than the market can provide in terms of quantitative goods, quantitative goods can become too short. The goods suppliers can then raise prices disproportionately. If money income is greatly increased and at the same time prices are increased accordingly, the supply situation of the participants does not improve. Hence, the value of money does not increase if people cannot buy more for correspondingly more money if prices rise.

If some people have no income but live on saved money, they can only buy goods to a decreasing extent when prices rise. The saved money then loses its value. If the loss in value becomes too great, the savers' confidence in the stability of the value of money will fade.

If other people earn their living with the help of state aid payments, for example, and these do not increase accordingly when prices rise, such people can only buy goods to a decreasing extent. Their supply situation deteriorates. These people also lose confidence in the stability of the value of money.

The above examples show that the extent of money withdrawal for the purpose of acquiring goods should not be oriented towards disproportionately high desires for money, because the sum of fulfilled desires for money can endanger the stability of the value of money too much for many people. Instead, the flow of goods and the flow of money should be coordinated in real economic cycles.

D 2   Quantitative real economic growth and qualitative growth

Quantitative growth in the real economy often involves an increase in workers' incomes. The increase in the production of goods takes place with the help of machinery and external energy input rather than by using human energy and the expenditure of human labor time. This means that as earnings rise, the workload for workers does not necessarily have to increase because the increase in the production of goods required for real economic growth is more likely to be provided by machinery and energy input than by human labor.

Workers can even expand qualitative aspects of working life such as holidays, breaks and a well-tolerable workload as their earnings rise. This is especially true as long as quantitative growth in the real economy prevails and ensures that the available labor is scarce. Workers can then, if they are dissatisfied with the distribution of qualitative aspects of working life, simply switch from one company to another that better fulfils their wishes for qualitative aspects of working life.

Holidays, breaks and well-tolerable workloads contribute to the quality of life of workers. They are qualitative goods. For employees, they offer free space and reduced workloads so that they can realize additional qualitative goods when living together with other people. This means that with quantitative growth in the real economy and increasing earnings, the amount of qualitative goods in the professional and private sphere can also increase.

Companies, however, are quantitatively burdened by the costs incurred for improving the quality of life of employees. If employers do not meet employees' demands for an increase in income or for an improvement in the quality of working life to a reasonable extent, they must expect that employees will switch to a competitor company that meets the employees' demands and can thus better exploit market opportunities.

With sufficient growth in the real economy, the increase in incomes and qualitative goods can take place in parallel. The state can also carry out its community tasks. This development is possible as long as the sum of all growth gains is sufficient to serve all participants, the employees, the employers and the state as the executor of the common tasks.

D 3   Quantitative real economic growth - Stability and democracy

At the beginning, we described barter relations as the basis of human cohabitation. Quantitative goods are exchanged for money and qualitative goods are bartered against each other.

If the quantitative real economy is interested in obtaining scarce quantitative goods and also in obtaining scarce money, the conditions for competition between suppliers and demanders are given. In order to achieve an advantage through competition, it is often important to be able to profit from knowledge advantages, exclusive information, involvement in interest groups, the secrecy of one's own knowledge or one's own experience. Competition takes place on the market.

Many market participants want to acquire the largest possible share of quantitative goods and money in order to survive, live comfortably, show off acquired status symbols and secure their future.

     2024-05-26

Market members can, of course, lose in competition with others, but they can also win. These aspects will be examined in the following.

-       Minimizing losses in the real economy with sufficient growth
Competition for quantitative goods and for money causes not only the hardship of losing but also the drive for all participants to obtain more. In the process, quantitative real economic growth is driven and the sum of growth successes can, in the course of time, bring about sufficient quantitative real economic growth. The opportunities for participation then increase for all market participants. In parallel, the number of losers in the race for participation is then minimized and most people are then apparently satisfied with the general situation.

The non-quantitative parts of human coexistence are very large as a sum. They ultimately include all components of human coexistence that money cannot or will not buy. These are the qualitative goods.

It is assumed that members of a society are satisfied if the survival and life of the individual is adequately secured and the incomes of different social classes do not diverge too much. Furthermore, it also seems important that the members of a society are satisfied with the mix of quantitative and qualitative goods they receive in the distribution process.

If there is sufficient quantitative growth in the real economy, people can be attracted to the idea of competing with others to obtain more and more quantitative goods and, at the same time, a sufficient level of quality of life.

-       Percentage increases in the distribution of growth gains
        when there is sufficient growth
As a consequence of quantitative real economic growth, growth gains can be distributed. These are increases in wages, salaries

and profits, for example. The increases often take place on a percentage basis. People with, for example, a high salary then receive a higher supplement than people with a small salary. This means that the gap between the incomes received is widening. People with higher incomes have a vested interest in maintaining such a percentage-based system, because they benefit from it.

As long as there is sufficient quantitative growth in the real economy, social stability as the basis for a democratic society should be guaranteed if the gap between high and low incomes does not widen too much, so that the difference can serve as an incentive for all those involved to want to receive more themselves. The difference should at least be perceived as fair and acceptable.

At the same time, the possibility of realizing an adequate quality of life should not be obstructed.

D 4   Exchanges of qualitative goods - stability of barter societies

When qualitative goods are exchanged on a large scale, this can lead to a breakdown of trust in the mutual balancing of inputs. As a result, tensions and instabilities can arise between the exchange partners.

Therefore, it seems logical for barter societies to achieve social stability through accompanying procedures.

In tribal societies, for example, social stability can be guaranteed by hierarchies with graded positional power and their traditional acceptance.

However, social stability is sometimes also realized through authoritarian procedures. Upper hierarchical levels often gain greater advantages than lower hierarchical levels. They thus have an interest in maintaining a stable form of society that is advantageous for them.

Power elites and power structures based on authoritarianism are accepted by more democratically organized interest groups in other countries to initiate, stabilize and secure economic relations with them. Cooperation with more authoritarian governments makes it unnecessary for interest groups of more democratic countries to forego their own advantages in favor of the poor population of more authoritarian states. However, this also makes it unnecessary to build a foundation for democratically based governments as alternatives to authoritarian governments.

When there are international protests against authoritarian states, the authoritarian style of government is the main target. Widespread existential poverty as a background to authoritarian societies tends not to be the subject of measures.

If the causes of poverty in interaction with authoritarian governments or countries that are becoming ungovernable were to be approached preventively to create a basis for democratic forms of government, this could suggest that redistribution of current account surpluses would be necessary. The politicians and governments involved obviously fear this kind of redistribution to the detriment of countries with current account surpluses. This may be because of the lack of acceptance by the people of the countries with current account surpluses.

D 5   Summary: The real economy and its players

Criteria are assembled which, given sufficient real economic growth, make the personal satisfaction of the individual members of a society, real economic stability and a democratic state possible:

- The members of a society should be able to participate satisfactorily in the growth gains. They should limit each other in terms of enforcing demands for growth gains in a way that creates stability.
- In parallel, there should be an increase in income, quantitative goods and qualitative goods. The state should take care of the common tasks to the required extent.
- In the race to share in growth gains, the number of losers should be minimized. Almost all members of a society should be able to participate in the growth gains to a sufficient extent. People's incomes should not diverge too excessively. Their difference should be surmountable or at least well acceptable. It should be possible to perceive them as fair in terms of performance.
- At least before growth gains become too low, before the members of a society become dissatisfied, before poor states are governed in an authoritarian manner, or very poor states even become ungovernable, appropriate prevention options should be considered.

E   Limits of the real economic drivers in case of quantitative real economic growth

Up to this point, we have shown the interaction between quantitative real economic growth spurred by various real economic drivers, the satisfaction of individual members of society, societal stability and democracy.

The drives for the realization of quantitative real economic growth described above have varying degrees of effectiveness and persistence. Therefore, they can also influence the interplay described above in different ways.

In this context, we will examine how the various drivers of the real economy reach the limits of their effectiveness, how quantitative growth in the real economy reaches its limits and how its interaction with social stability and democracy can be influenced.

E 1   Limits of the real economic driver "Quantitative goods"

People's needs and desires and the resulting demands are a driver for the acquisition of quantitative goods. Needs are at the heart of a real economy. To pay for the goods, money is used. Quantitative goods and money form real economy cycles. The goods flow in one direction and the money flows in the opposite direction to pay for them. The money for paying the goods is earned, among other things, by producing quantitative goods.

It seems that especially the desires to obtain quantitative goods know hardly any limits. They are potentially capable of acting as drivers of permanent quantitative real economic growth. However, the fulfilment of desires obviously has its limits. These are described below.

- Lack of money impedes quantitative growth in the real economy

There are people who have too little money for sufficient or even comfortable participation in real economic cycles. This lack of money may, for example, occur as a result of unemployment due to automation and rationalization. However, it may also mean that some people have too little money at their disposal because they receive only very small supplements in percentage income increases compared to people who earn well. On a global scale, some people never have the chance to receive a sufficient amount of money. Lack of money and thus lack of purchasing power can thus hinder quantitative real economic growth.

- Saving impedes quantitative real economic growth

Apart from rather poor people with low incomes, there are also people with high incomes. Particularly these people do not spend all their money on consumer goods. They then have money left over to save. First, the money saved can be used for investment. If the productivity in the production of goods becomes so high with the help of corresponding investments that the additionally produced consumer goods are no longer needed for increasing consumption, then the need for investment and the money saved for it will decrease. The money that is still saved will be withdrawn from the real economic cycles because it will not be used again in a growth-oriented manner for the acquisition of consumption or investment goods. Saving can thus impede quantitative growth in the real economy.

- Limited resources impede quantitative real economic growth

In addition to the influence of money, consumer goods and capital goods on quantitative real economic growth, there is also the influence of limited resources such as raw materials, energy and the exhaustible environment. If the resources required for the production of quantitative goods become scarcer and more expensive or are even lacking in the real economy, this can also impede quantitative real economic growth.

84

E 2 Limits of the real economic driver "Manpower requirements"

If people were not assisted by energy, machinery, automata or information technology in their provision of goods, their limited physical capacity and working time would let them be largely occupied with fundamental life-sustaining provision of goods.

When workers are supported by energy, machinery, automata or information technology, their efficiency in producing goods improves. They can produce more and more goods. This makes quantitative real economic growth possible, provided that workers receive corresponding increases in income and there are enough unfulfilled desires.

If this growth is combined with the interests of people with greater financial assets, and profit-oriented investments in machinery and automatization are made, the realigned increase of efficient goods production will lead to less labor needed to produce the quantitative goods offered for sale. The released labor capacities can then increasingly be used for producing effective machinery and automation to strengthen real economic growth through more production.

- Limits

At a certain point in this development, the production of quantitative goods by means of automated production plants and rationalization releases more labor than needed for producing more consumer goods and making new investments Insofar as released workers become unemployed in an oversupply on the labor market or earn less money in later jobs, they have less purchasing power at their disposal. Quantitative growth in the real economy is thus weakened because less can be bought.

Against this background, the generation of real economic growth with the help of automation and rationalization can turn into the opposite at a certain point. Then, the conditions for quantitative real economic growth are fulfilled to a decreasing extent because, on the one hand, the supply of quantitative goods can increase due to automation and, on the other hand, the purchasing power of lower earning or no longer needed workers will decrease. Thus, the conditions for quantitative growth in the real economy are fulfilled to a decreasing extent. These require not only an increase in the supply of goods but also an increase in income. Both increases should be coordinated and characterized by shortages

E 3   Limits of the real economic driver "Current account surplus"

Current account surplus means that loans granted for this purpose earn interest. On the other hand, a current account deficit means that interest has to be paid in addition to the repayment of the loans taken out.

-      Limits

If repayments plus interest payments become too high for countries with a current account deficit, these countries may have to be relieved of their debts so that they can continue to import goods and do not become deficient as trading partner.

--   Debt relief for over-indebted trading partners means, on the other hand, an indirect negative impact on the quantitative real economic growth of countries with a current account surplus.

--   Furthermore, in over-indebted countries, debt repayment plus interest payments can lead to heavy financial burdens and social unrest.

E 4 Limits of the real economic driver "Waste of goods"

The money for producing goods such as food, which are later wasted because of their limited durability, has to be raised by selling other goods. Avoiding the waste would allow the money saved to be used for other purposes. It could strengthen alternative drivers of the real economy.

The following measures can be taken to avoid waste:
Consumers can purchase their goods without giving priority to those with the longest durability, which helps to reduce the risk of waste.

Manufacturers can adjust production planning and logistics in a way that reduces waste.

In reality, there is a considerable amount of waste. In other words, the sum of individual and corporate behavior causes the waste problem, which increases the scarcity of resources.

E 5 Limits of the real economic driver "Resource consumption"

During the production of quantitative goods, resources such as raw materials, energy and the environment are consumed. If the demand for quantitative goods increases substantially, this means at first glance a corresponding increase in the demand for resources. In this way, the livelihood of people can be greatly reduced.

However, technical progress makes the manufacture of products increasingly economical in terms of resources. This can be clearly seen, for example, if we imagine the resource requirements for the production of a precision mechanical machine control and compare this with the production of an IT control with the same range of functions.

The resource requirements for individual functional units have thus often decreased considerably over time. However, it is decisive for the resource requirement whether the number of functional units used per product increases over time, as the products become more and more convenient and complex. Furthermore, resource requirements are characterized by the increase in purchased goods - such as technical devices.

If the demand for functional units and products increases greatly, the absolute demand for resources increases above a certain growth level despite savings in the individual functional unit.

-     Limits
It is evident that in the case of permanent quantitative real economic growth, ultimately infinite quantities of resources such as raw materials, energy and the environment are required. However, these are not available in unlimited quantities.

To differentiate, it should be noted that, for example, the abundant resource of non-renewable energy is indirectly limited in its use. The limitation is revealed by the fact that their use causes too much damage to the limited environment available.

The capacity of renewable energy is ultimately limited by the need for sites and raw materials for the energy supply facilities.

E 6   Limits of the real economic driver "Innovative products"

Innovative products can serve to offer people opportunities to improve their standard of living. Thus, the market for innovative products could actually grow continuously.

- Limits

In the course of time, social groups may arise that get too little money to afford a much better standard of living by means of innovative products beyond the satisfaction of basic needs.

E 7 Limits of the real economic driver „Status gain"

Status gain can be achieved when people receive attention and recognition through the purchase of status goods. At first glance, it seems feasible that people would want to continuously increase the acquisition of status goods. In this way, they would permanently stimulate quantitative real economic growth.

As the development of the real economy shows, in the distribution of scarce financial resources over time, advantages for some population groups are achieved at the expense of other population groups. On the one hand, money resources then increase and, on the other hand, purchasing power tends to be weakened.

People who have little money quickly spend it again to cover their basic needs. If their purchasing power tends to decrease, they can also buy fewer goods.

People who have more and more money at their disposal often do not spend the increase to the same extent on status goods and status gain - they also save and thus withdraw money from the real economy.

- Limits

The shift in the receipt of money from poorer to richer segments of the population can thus lead to a weakening of growth, because some receive and can spend less money and others spend only part of the additional money on additional status goods in order to save the rest.

E 8   Limits of the real economic drivers: "Environmental protection, use of renewable energy and recycling"

The use of resources creates a scarcity of resources. Recycling, the use of renewable energy and environmental protection can reduce this scarcity. In this way, the period of resource use can be extended. This is an important aspect of sustainability.

-     Limits

The shortage of raw materials is closely related to recycling, the provision of renewable energy and environmental protection. The more money is used to secure the future for innovative technologies, recycling, the provision of renewable energy and environmental protection, the more money would actually have to be withdrawn from other real economic cycles, e.g. for consumption. This is especially true where the state carries out recycling, provision of renewable energy and environmental protection as community tasks and finances them through redistribution. The state's activity becomes more urgent where individuals push recycling, provision of renewable energy and environmental protection into the background for their own benefit, e.g. by purchasing non-sustainable goods.

Technical progress involving the development of technologies for recycling, renewable energy and environmental protection improves export opportunities. However, increasing exports can lead to burdens in countries with current account deficits.

E 9   Limits of real economic driver „Investments"

Investments serve, among other things, to finance production facilities that can be used to cover the demand for goods. By means of energy, machinery and automation, the productivity of such plants can be improved. This development is specifically rein-forced by the exploitation interest of those investors who primarily want to increase their money through rationalization.

First of all, real economic cycles can be driven by increased productivity, increasing profits of enterprises and increasing earn-ings of workers.

- Limits

As soon as increased productivity frees up labor that is no longer needed for the production of consumer goods and production fa-cilities, their incomes often fall and with them the general pur-chasing power. This development weakens real economic cycles, which means that fewer investments are required.

E 10 Limits of the real economic driver „Education"

Education has two key areas.

The first is general education, which is part of general social life.

Secondly, education serves the realization of research, develop-ment, technical progress, innovative products, automation and or-ganization. It is thus a driver of real economic growth, although its effect is rather delayed.

- Limits

Firstly, payment for education is part of the state's common tasks and thus dependent on the financial possibilities of the state.

Secondly, education is also financed by companies, and this ed-ucation is then primarily oriented towards the exploitation inter-ests of the companies. Education precedes real economic growth as a precursor to research, development, technical progress, in-novative products, automation and effective organization. The in-terest of companies in paying for education specifically requires that education, within its preliminary period, should be designed for calculable periods of time and for growth in the real economy.

Education has countervailing effects:

Education, training, knowledge, research and development are important prerequisites for technical progress. They increase the amplification factor of human performance. Together with automation and rationalization, this can increase the productivity of the production of goods.

Initially, education is a driver of quantitative real economic growth from which almost everyone can benefit.

Over time, fewer people are needed for the production of goods because their education-supported reinforcement factor and their productivity increase. Thus, as productivity increases, a decreasing number of people can provide increasingly more quantitative goods. This leads to a decreasing number of people having enough money to buy manufactured goods in sufficient quantities. This provokes the weakening of quantitative real economic growth.

Education can thus influence quantitative real economic growth in two ways. First, growth can increase. Second, it can weaken.

A further consideration shows that education, training, knowledge, research and development can on the one hand serve the purpose of achieving primarily short-term successes in a real economy, but on the other hand they can also serve the purpose of sustainability in a real economy. Both purposes differ in the aspect of time.
- Therefore, on the one hand, there is the human ambition to generate as much additional money as possible by using money, automation and rationalization in the real economy and to do this by producing goods in the shortest possible

time. The cycle of money use should be as short as possible, i.e. the money shall circulate at a high speed. Each cycle should create additional money. The circulation rate can be reinforced using the information technology as a part of the technological progress. This leads to an increasing production of goods and consumption of resources.

-   On the other hand, when using money, we should strive for the longest possible periods of use for human labor, manufactured goods and resources - for the purpose of sustainability.

It can be seen that time plays an important role when considering real economic development from the perspective of education.

On the one hand, the use of money in the real economy can be about education-supported short-term success. This success should be able to be repeated as quickly as possible with each renewed use of money. With each renewed real economy-based use of money, resources are also needed. This reduces their availability.

However, the focus lies on a long-term, education-based sustainability to secure resources.

E 11 Limits of the real economic drivers: "Savings, loans and money given directly to companies"

Saving money or its subsequent use takes place in different contexts, such as, for example, the following

-   Saving after covering the need for quantitative goods
-   Saving, e.g. for the planned purchase of a car or a house.
-   Saving as a precaution for future uncertainties
-   Saving for retirement provision
-   Saving as a provision for future generations

When money is saved, it is at first sight withdrawn from the real economic cycles, unless banks lend the savings deposited with them to consumers or companies or savers give their money to companies, e.g. by buying shares.
-     Limits
In summary, if the sum of savings is much larger than the sum of loans granted, including savings granted directly to enterprises, this indicates a weakening of the real economy.

E 12   Limits of the real economic driver "Redistribution for the fulfilment of community tasks"

On the one hand, it seems logical that the fulfilment of common tasks should be carried out equally by all members of society, because they also tend to benefit equally from them.

On the other hand, it seems logical to take the money for redistribution towards the fulfilment of community tasks away from the people who do not currently want to use it.

If the redistribution funds are withdrawn fairly equally from all members of society and if the money flows quickly back into the real economic cycles after redistribution, redistribution tends to have a neutral effect on growth,

If the money is primarily withdrawn from those who do not currently need it and want to use it, and if the redistributed funds are quickly returned to the real economy, redistribution tends to promote growth.

-     Limits
Against this background, the state's redistribution policy can be used to steer growth.

2024-05-26

If the amount of money redistributed in the direction of common tasks becomes greater than the growth gains as a whole, there is a need for government debt. This development requires closer examination later.

E 13   Summary: Limits of the efficiency of real economic drivers

Having shown that human relationships can be represented by describing their exchange relationships with qualitative and quantitative goods and that increasing desires to meet human needs can be satisfied, e.g., by increasing quantitative real economic growth, the issue arises as to the consistency of growth. Therefore, limits to quantitative growth in the real economy are considered.

All drivers of quantitative real economic growth should realize sufficient quantitative real economic growth in order to enable social satisfaction through the distribution of growth gains. If real economic drivers reach the limits of their constancy and if growth gains become too low, those involved would have to forego growth gains or even accept a reduction. However, as experience shows, most members of a society are at least interested in preserving their vested rights.

If permanent quantitative growth in the real economy is required as the basis of a stable democratic state, but cannot be guaranteed, the crucial question of the interplay between inadequate growth in the real economy and the stability of a democracy arises.

This begs the question for measures to counteract the weakness of quantitative real economic growth. To this end, we consider strategies that can be used to postpone limits to the consistency of real economic drivers.

F Impacting the efficiency limits of real economy drivers

A permanently effective strategy to prevent deficient quantitative real economic growth would require to be able to postpone or even remove obviously existing limits to the effectiveness of real economic drivers.

Before considering this strategy, we will examine the question whether there is a need for permanent quantitative growth in the real economy. If we could do without this kind of growth, we would not need strategies to counteract the limiting effects of real economic drivers.

At first glance, quantitative real economic growth seems to be necessary. This theory is based on the fact that especially in industrialized countries, the demand for permanent quantitative growth in the real economy is made when it comes to combat deficiencies in the real economy. When people demand permanent quantitative growth to combat deficiencies in the real economy, they obviously fail to consider that growth does not necessarily result in eliminating deficiencies in the real economy. When influenced by special interests in the real economy, their use can also lead to an increase in real economic and ecological deficiencies. Where might the demand for permanent quantitative real economic growth come from, if it is made despite possible failures?

Making survival possible is a logical central interest for humans. In cold climates, stockpiling was very useful for this purpose already in early times. To realize them, they developed their planning and organizing skills. Thus, in more cold climates, nature teaches people to plan and organize their food storage. In this way, survival could be increasingly better ensured.

The experience of planning and organizing patterned future behavior. This improved the possibilities for satisfying needs and increasing the quality of life beyond survival.

Human behavior shows that people are hardly willing to forego an increasingly better standard of living with the help of quantitative growth in the real economy. Thus, the focus is on how to influence deficient quantitative real economic growth, how to postpone obviously existing growth limits or how to perhaps even dismantle them.

F 1   Impacting the efficiency limits of the real economy driver "Quantitative goods"

If a part of the population saves too much money or if other people have too little money available, then they can buy correspondingly fewer goods.

Savings can be caused by people being able to meet their basic needs and comfort requirements without having to use all of their income to do so. At the same time, as the real economy develops, there may be an increasing number of people who, for example due to unemployment, have too little money to buy goods beyond a minimum requirement.

In each case, the acquisition of goods is reduced because less money is spent or can be spent on them. Real economic cycles are weakened in terms of money and the acquisition of goods. There are less growth gains available to be distributed.

However, if the members of a society are accustomed to get permanent growth gains, they might become discontent if these gains are lacking. Since politicians wish that people are satisfied because they want to be reelected, they try to prevent a lack of quantitative real economic growth.

This might be achieved if the government redistributes money from people with larger savings to those with too low incomes, thus enabling additional quantitative real economic growth.

To avoid the resistance of people with larger savings, but at the same time preventing a weakening of quantitative real economic growth, the state often provides aid through subsidies or transfer payments. The money is supposed to increase purchasing possibilities and boost real-economy cycles.

- Limits

If growth gains are too low to provide the state with the money needed for aid payments, politicians might try to get the necessary money as a loan or credit and thus indebting the state. In doing so, they promise to repay the loans later when there is sufficient real-economy growth. But experience shows that the repayment of the loans taken out to finance national debts is made in insufficient amounts. If the national debt then becomes too large, the extent to which the real economic driver "quantitative goods" can be influenced by aid payments reaches its limit.

F 2   Impacting the efficiency limits of the real economy driver "Labor force"

As long as there is sufficient quantitative real-economic growth by producing and selling quantitative goods and almost all people have sufficiently well-paid jobs, the real economic situation appears to be stable.

As automation and rationalization proceed, labor forces are set free in the production process of consumer goods and can initially be used to realize further automation and rationalization. But thus, the production of consumer and capital goods becomes increasingly more and more effective, and the released labor forces are then needed to a lesser and lesser extent. Their income is often lower in subsequent jobs, or they become unemployed and receive a smaller amount as assistance. This development is outlined below.

F 2.1   Low paid activities

If unemployment arises, it often results in low-paid work. It can be seen, for example, in service activities for private individuals, non-industrial activities and industrial activities. These activity variants are examined in more detail below.

-    Low paid services for individuals
With the development of the real economy, some people are increasingly achieving good incomes. They often have too little time to settle their private affairs. These people then have service tasks to assign but cannot or do not want to pay enough money for it so that the payees can live sufficiently well from it.

To fulfill these insufficiently paid services, they often hire people who have become unemployed due to automation and rationalization and who cannot keep up in the competitive race for well-paid jobs.

The interaction of high earners and low earners can be fanned out as follows.

In times of sufficient quantitative real-economy growth and adequate leisure time, well-off people can also be well provided for with qualitative goods such as mutual service.

If the compression of work and the expansion of working hours increase for high-earners due to insufficient quantitative real-economy growth and increasing rationalization, there will be less space for exchanging qualitative goods, such as mutual service, for them. Thus, if there is a lack of time for mutual rendering of gratuitous service, it must be paid for it.

During periods of deficient quantitative real-economy growth, services tend to be low-paid because there is an oversupply of labor forces for rendering them. These people's low employment opportunities are caused by the rationalization-oriented activity of the people, who then appear as demanders for low-paid service.

In this context, it seems sensible to avoid low charges for services and to prescribe appropriate remuneration. This should enable the receiving people to realize an adequate standard of living and a retirement provision that prevents old-age poverty. Consequently, the recipients of the service would have to pay the higher fees for the service performers or they would have to do the work themselves. Then the workload, the compression of work, the free spaces, and the remuneration for potential service recipients would have to be readjusted. The vested interests of some service recipients obviously successfully prevent such a development, so that there are people who can hardly make a decent living, who are threatened with old-age poverty and who may form a trouble potential for the future.

-    Low paid non-industrial activities
In addition to the rather poorly remunerated service tasks in the private sector, there are also insufficiently remunerated tasks in various non-industrial sectors such as agriculture, gastronomic service, hairdressing, and so on. Two aspects are considered in this regard. First, it is the corrective leveling between increased incomes to be prescribed and resulting prices. Secondly, the role of personal responsibility is considered.

Corrective leveling between income and prices:
An appropriately increased remuneration that ensures livelihood and retirement for low-income people would require price increases for goods and services produced or rendered by those people. This would have consequences.

On the one hand, the low paid people would have to be able to pay the prices that were raised for their benefit. Therefore, the wages and salaries of these people would have to be increased to the extent that this is also possible

On the other hand, the increased prices would have to be paid in particular by people with good incomes. They might then save less money or purchase slightly fewer comfort goods.

The corrective leveling between increased wages and salaries on the one hand and the resulting prices on the other would cause a redistribution that would counteract the weakening of a real economy by partly too low purchasing power due to o the insufficient remuneration of some people.

Role of personal responsibility:
People with well-established incomes can make themselves appear more capable because they can afford more than poorer people due to their higher incomes.

They may refer to personal responsibility for income as a reason for high incomes, although these are often fixed by collective agreements.

For those with higher incomes, the concept of personal responsibility might also be attractive because they could use it to justify their own higher incomes, although these incomes leave a rather too small share for other people from the income group.

According to the logic of personal responsibility for high-income earners, low-income earners are also responsible for their low earnings, because these would logically have to be a reflection of lower efficiency.

As a part of the personal responsibility for income, high-income earners can also reject higher prices if they are used to improve especially the remuneration of low-income earners.

In deviation from what is presumably perceived as personal responsibility for some incomes, the level of incomes up to a certain level is often determined by distributional modes such as collective bargaining and legislation. Distributional modes for low and high-income people are more likely to be determined by higher-income people because they are more likely to be opinionated. Thus, it can be explained that people with higher incomes favor themselves with higher supplements because they prefer a proportional distribution with income increases. In this respect, it must be explicitly outlined here that higher incomes receive a higher supplement than lower incomes in the case of proportional increases. With this in mind, the permanent divergence of incomes in favor of those with higher incomes is often concealed under the pretext of personal responsibility.

-       Low-paid industrial activities
First, there are jobs in industrialized countries that, once salaries and wages are increased, can no longer compete in cost terms with those in low-wage countries. These increases can lead to the relocation of the production of goods and the associated jobs to countries with low wages. In industrialized countries, this often affects the jobs of rather low-skilled people. As a result, some people who have become unemployed only get low-paying jobs, so that their livelihood is often no longer adequately guaranteed.

Second, the increase in wages and salaries is largely proportional. As a result, the income gap is widening. People with higher incomes receive a larger amount as a supplement than those people with lower incomes when their percentage increases. Because of the income gap effect, more and more people with low incomes can no longer adequately cover their living expenses.

Increasing wages and salaries in industrialized countries can lead to an increasing number of people being unable to earn an adequate living in these countries because their jobs are relocated to low-wage countries as a result of it and incomes tend to fall.

The proportional increase in wages and salaries can also widen the income gap to such an extent that some people will no longer have enough money because their incomes remain too low.

The considerations above lead to the idea of representing global income development as the following staircase:

First, industrialized countries show incomes that allow for a good and comfortable life.

Second, there are incomes in industrialized countries that are too low to provide a decent living. This comprises incomes in the private service sector, in the non-industrial sector and in the industrial sector.

Third, in industrialized countries, low-paid people receive enough support to ensure a minimum level of care.

Fourth, goods are produced in barely industrialized countries for very low wages, which people with too low incomes in industrialized countries can also afford. Thus, people in industrialized countries can obviously be supplied with supplementary products from low-wage countries to such an extent that industrialized countries do not have to fear social unrest because their inhabitants are too poorly supplied with low-income products.

Fifth, low wages in non-industrialized countries are so low that very many people live at minimum subsistence levels. They hardly have enough money to build up a base of savings. If they have no health insurance, they can hardly pay for the necessary medicine in case of illness. In traditional communities, people support each other; they are often obligated to do so. For such purposes, any savings are used then, animals are sold or wages are paid in advance. These people subsidize people in rich countries through their low incomes.

Sixth, people die as a result of insufficient existential care.

Countries that are hardly industrialized have little chance of getting on a growth path that could bring them sufficient growth gains and social stability based on them.

The staircase symbolizes the supply of people with goods and money. The lowest levels represent hunger and low wages, and are obviously necessary so that people with too low incomes in industrialized countries can afford enough goods from low-wage countries to avoid meltdowns in potential trouble spots in industrialized countries.

F 2.2　　Low paid skills

At times of insufficient quantitative real-economy growth, the trend toward low remuneration primarily affects those employment sectors that require only low qualifications and for which there is an oversupply of labor forces. Even qualified people can get caught in the vicious circle of low pay if their skills are not or no longer needed. This is, for example, the case if, as experienced personnel, they can be replaced by other people who can perform given tasks with less experience with the help of IT-based knowledge and who therefore have lower income expectations

In a first approach, it can be supposed that if there is an oversupply of labor forces, their income is in a similar way too high as the supply of labor is too large. However, this is not the case. On the contrary, employers can disproportionately reduce their income offer, accompanied by the comment, not necessarily to be uttered, that other workers would work for it. Incomes are often so low that the people concerned can hardly cover their basic needs from the income generated.

In response to too low incomes, employers might try to raise their product prices to the point where they could pay their workers high enough wages that they would be able to support themselves in an adequate manner. These employers then rely on their customers being willing to pay higher prices for the known purpose. Without this willingness, there is a risk that these employers will be forced out of the market by competitors with lower prices and lower wages and salaries.

The real market has not yet produced a significant trend towards higher prices for the purpose of higher incomes for underpaid workers.

Apparently, there is no self-dynamic development in the direction of preventing the impoverishment of population groups. The phenomenon of impoverishment can be observed when there is unemployment among a considerable group of people or when incomes tend to fall.

If a self-dynamic development were possible that prevented the impoverishment of population groups through too low incomes at times of insufficient quantitative real-economy growth, then it would already have been apparent. To make such a development possible, the prices for the goods produced by these people would have had to increase to the extent necessary to raise incomes adequately. The competition for customers, who are or have to be oriented towards the lowest price level, seems to significantly prevent such a development.

F 2.3   Individual behavior and societal development

We will consider individual behavior, sufficient or weakening real-economy growth, polarization, advantage and disadvantage.

- Sufficient quantitative real-economy growth

There are times of real economic development when almost all people in a society can increasingly cover their needs. However, this seems to require that the production of goods, demand for goods, employment, income and profits can and do increase step by step. The members of the society then obviously trust that such a development will continue automatically and result in sufficient quantitative real-economy growth and remain unchanged. The trust in such processes is confirmed again and again as if by magic. There are continuously increasing growth gains in store for almost everyone involved. These gains allow individual satisfaction for many people and the fulfilment of community tasks by the state - with participation and at the expense of those involved. This builds a foundation for social stability and democracy.

However, a continued sufficient quantitative real-economy growth requires that resources such as energy, raw materials and the environment are still available for consumption.

Machinery and information technology are also important. They are created by humans and can reinforce human action.

We have shown in the previous presentation the central elements for sufficient quantitative real-economy growth.

As a next step, we will first explain how sufficient quantitative real-economy growth can falter and what could be done about it.

- Weakening quantitative real-economy growth

As soon as quantitative real-economy growth weakens, e.g. because the purchasing power of a large number of people decreases to the advantage of people who save their money, the distribution of growth gains would have to be changed in favor of people with too small incomes to ensure that growth remains possible.

The distribution to the people with too little money could be done in such a way that in distributing growth gains with more equal distribution, they receive increasing supplements and the people with large incomes receive decreasing supplements. In this way, the poorer people could quickly return their increased income to real economic cycles and stimulate growth by covering their existing needs. People with higher incomes would receive decreasing supplements if growth gains were more equally distributed, and thus less money to save and withdraw from real economic cycles.

The change in the distribution of income could alternatively be initiated by mandating reasonably higher wages to be received by those on low incomes. The higher prices of goods resulting from higher incomes would primarily burden the people with higher incomes, who would then be able to save less, while for the poorer people incomes would have to rise so much that they could also adequately compensate for the price increases. This process represents a growth-oriented redistribution from richer to poorer people.

-       Polarized incomes - Advantaged - Disadvantaged
In times of weakening quantitative real-economy growth, sufficient redistribution in favor of people with too low incomes for the purpose of permanent quantitative real-economy growth does not seem to be an automatic development. If redistribution were a self-fulfilling process, it would have shown itself by now. On the contrary - the distribution of growth gains, when primarily distributed as a proportion, results in people with higher incomes receiving a larger supplement than those with lower incomes. Considering this, people with higher incomes are more likely to save than people with lower incomes, who are more likely to lack money to ensure a decent living. When incomes are increased in proportion, those with higher incomes appear to benefit at the expense of those who benefit to a lesser extent from the growth gains.

When distributing growth gains, it is obviously not possible for well-intentioned beneficiaries of real economic development to change the distribution key in favor of disadvantaged population groups to a relevant extent in order to reduce societal polarization. They obviously cannot achieve that most people with higher incomes do the same.

-       Polarizations and variants of growth
At times of sufficient quantitative real economic growth, there can be a self-dynamic development of the increase in income as long as all parties involved can trust that income, purchasing power, production of goods, acquisition of goods and profits will gradually increase continuously.

In the period of insufficient quantitative real economic growth and emerging social polarization, we observe market failures, both on the part of employers and employees - as shown below:

- If employers raise the prices of their products in favor of higher wages for the low-paid, they must expect that a significant proportion of competitors will not do so and will drive them out of the market.

- If beneficiaries on the employee side forego the distribution of growth gains in favor of the low-paid, they cannot count on a substantial number of other beneficiaries doing the same. Rather, it must be expected that other beneficiaries will take advantage of the waiver.

Once the transition from sufficient quantitative real economic growth to deficient quantitative real economic growth has been made, polarization and market failures become evident. What remains, however, is an expectation that a market should be used to ensure that the people involved are sufficiently supplied with goods to be able to realize an adequate standard of living. Often, when the expectation of a good supply of goods, social polarization and obvious market failures coincide, aid payments are made to prevent social discontent.

- Limits of support for insufficient income
Some industrialized countries provide public assistance to people with insufficient income. This may be done for moral reasons or to dampen dissatisfaction with the state.

Once they reach a certain level, support payments can become so large that the real economic cycles can no longer provide them adequately because they would be bled dry. Then the state is tempted to procure the necessary money through national debt. The government keeps support payments relatively low for a variety of reasons.

First, the state keeps support payments low under the pretext of maintaining an incentive for workers to strive for higher incomes. This approach means for many people that although they have a full-time job, their income is not sufficient to adequately cover their basic needs and secure their future through pensions.

Second, there are the more younger people who will have to pay down the national debt later. Their logical interest is to minimize the amount of current borrowing for the purpose of helping people with insufficient income.

Third, the government wants to maintain, with rather little support of the low-income earners, the goodwill of people whose high incomes could increasingly be used for redistribution to low-income earners.

Finally, the different interests regarding the support of people with too low-income result in the fact that the support is quite limited. In this context, some people may be tempted to engage in a so-called "discussion of values" about alternative values that are to be realized through volunteering. This work might be intended to help people acquire self-esteem and external recognition as alternative values in addition to low incomes, so that they do not end up in a state of dissatisfaction.

F 2.4   Volunteering

Volunteering exists, mutatis mutandis, in a variety of contexts.

-     Initially, mutual unpaid giving and taking is considered a form of volunteering.
--   These are, for example, mutual aids in tribal contexts where people depend on each other.
--   Helping one another takes on a special impetus when people are dependent on one another, for example, in crises and wars.
--   In times when the value of money is declining sharply, people often help each other to replace money as a medium of exchange.
--   Often there are friends, neighbors and acquaintances who help each other. In addition to the aspect of non-remuneration, these aids often also have a communicative aspect.

-     Volunteering in times of sufficient quantitative real economic growth

One interesting aspect seems to be that in times of sufficient quantitative growth in the real economy, mutual assistance seems to be particularly valued from a communication point of view. In the event of a shortage of labor forces, people will not only be able to push through increasingly higher wages and salaries, but can additionally maintain and expand qualitative aspects of reward at work through leisure time and limiting workload. This means that there is increasing private space for mutual help and communicative coexistence.

- Volunteering and weakening quantitative real economy

If quantitative growth in the real economy no longer yields sufficient growth gains for everyone, incomes tend to fall for some people and some other people become unemployed. Then mutual gratuitous help becomes meaningful, in order to compensate the lack of financial means for acquiring quantitative goods.

Furthermore, there is an interest on the part of the state to foster volunteering. This work might be intended to cover claims on the state regarding the fulfillment of community tasks. Volunteering then has the character of unilateral taking by the population, which is obviously not willing to pay the necessary taxes to pay for the completion of some community tasks.

Volunteering can be a way for unemployed people to gain social recognition and to enhance the meaning of their lives with it.

Representatives of the public might be tempted to create themselves an image as problem solvers in the completion of community tasks by supporting volunteering. Social institutions and nonprofit associations might be seduced by the temptation to have their image burnished by volunteers. Supporting this assumption is the natural interest of employees of such organizations to secure their paid jobs by organizing volunteering.

F 2.5   The denigration of people who are wrongly qualified

Low-skilled people and people with skills not needed in the real economy often receive low pay or the state provides them with a minimum of support. In conjunction with products from low-wage countries that are also affordable for them, these people can then make a living in such a way that they obviously do not form a potential for social unrest.

At the same time, there are successfully established people in the real economy who, through automation and rationalization, among other things, have made sure that low-skilled or incorrectly qualified people are needed and paid in insufficient numbers. In times of growth, people successfully established in the real economy often secured a share in the growing real economy by means of regulations to safeguard vested rights. In the event of later insufficient quantitative real economic growth, the established participation will still be gladly taken up, if necessary also at the detriment of people with low incomes. In times of sufficient real economic growth, successfully established people thus remain at least partial beneficiaries at the expense of people with too low incomes in times of insufficient real economic growth. If vested rights did not exist, the beneficiaries would presumably often have little chance of maintaining their income levels in the face of inadequate real economic growth.

When people who are not needed on the labor market in sufficient numbers and thus receive low pay demonstratively defend themselves against the consequences of social polarization and the preservation of vested interests, they are easily assigned the image of dumbasses or even dimwits due to their lack of or incorrect qualifications and education. Thus, it is easy to divert attention from the causes outlined above.

In combination with societal polarization, there are obviously people with too low incomes. In the competition to share in growth gains, they often find themselves on the road to hopelessness for long periods of time. If they resist, for example, by means of demonstrations, they are sometimes threatened with defamation. We should not underestimate the political explosive power of such a development.

However, the problem could be solved by the demographic development. This could be done by gradually replacing the diminishing majority of aging beneficiaries with a supermajority of disadvantaged and, above all, less polarizing people, who would reorganize the distribution in society on a democratic basis.

F 3 Impacting the efficiency limits of the real economy driver "Current account surplus" through export protection

Quantitative real economy growth can be boosted by export surpluses. This happens when, on the one hand, there are export surpluses and current account surpluses for exporting countries.

Then, on the other hand, importing countries with current account deficits have to repay the loans taken out to finance imports. Additionally, they have to pay the accruing interests.

In the context of international development, there are countries with a balanced current account. However, particularly competitive and less competitive countries are also emerging. Some may be characterized by accumulated current account surplus and others by current account deficit.

Countries with export surpluses face the risk of defaulting on incoming payments if payment uncertainty develops in countries with current account deficits as payment burdens increase. To make the resulting export risk calculable for companies, it is partly assumed by their home countries through export insurance.

The countries with current account deficits are at risk of overindebtedness, which could impose excessive burdens on society.

The government may be responsible for these burdens. That happens when it causes a negative current account balance through imports, which it then has to balance, including interest. He is most likely to get the money to pay for it from the public or businesses, thus burdening society.

However, the burden can also be caused by importing companies if they have to repay loans taken out for imports plus interest and can therefore only pay low wages and salaries.

- Limits

In countries with current account deficits, the burden of repaying loans, including interest, in parallel with the population's poor income situation can lead to social and political tensions. These developments can bring authoritarian governments or even ungovernability of countries for the purpose of maintaining stability.

With regard to authoritarian governments in poor states, demands for democratization and good governance are often made on such countries. However, it seems obvious that people in poor countries are more likely to recognize compliance with such demands as important if their survival is assured, they have enough to eat and they are provided with a fundamental health care system.

In various states we can observe ungovernability including its consequences such as war, war costs, suffering of the population and flight of the population. This includes integration costs for refugees in their host countries.

The manifestations of authoritarian governments and ungovernable states suggest that preventive action should be taken to counteract the causal undesirable developments in the real economy.

Longer-term real economic easing through current account equalization between poor and rich countries would presumably activate the real economic beneficiaries in the countries with current account surpluses as opponents.

F 4   "Doing something good" as a marketing strategy against waste of goods, but also a real economic driver

If the durability of food is no longer guaranteed, they are in danger of being wasted. Goods stored for this purpose are often donated, before they are wasted, to people who have too little money to cover their minimal needs.

For people who donate, doing "something good" for poor people by giving them food that is in danger of being destroyed has an image-enhancing effect. However, this transforms the annihilation problem into a behavioral problem.

First, the destruction of food is transformed into a donation of food. Second, however, the recipients of donations learn non-market behavior because they receive food paying for it. People who donate should not be surprised if they are increasingly met by such conditioned people with demands for services without anything in return. The behavior of people who donate encourages an economy of begging rather than a real economy in which all parties have to contribute appropriately to a functioning supply system.

Donating food, however, helps saving resources.

If food has to be donated or even wasted, these processes mean that it is still a real economic driver because the cost of producing it has to be paid additionally by regular buyers of food. This is how real economic cycles close.

F 5   Impacting the efficiency limits of the real economy driver "Resource consumption"

A growing real economy plausibly entails an increasing consumption of resources. Initially, the increase in consumption leads to a shortage of resources. In economic theory, this should increase the price of resources and thus not only reduce the demand for resources, but also the demand for goods produced with them, which would also become more expensive. However, the links between the growing real economy, the demand for resources, the goods produced with them, resource scarcity and resource prices are more diverse than initially might be assumed. To this end, the following considerations are made.

- Research and development allow resources to be used increasingly effectively. This has a compensating effect on their shortage and price increase.
- Research and development also lead to the production of new forms of energy. This also reduces shortages.
- Another phenomenon are subsidies for the extraction of resources. This can create additional capacity for resource extraction. Thus, over time, as supply increases, there may be downward pressure on resource prices. This process also affects the revenues of poor supplier countries that rely on resource export revenues.

Resource extraction is also characterized by the fact that people with low income levels in semi-industrialized countries provide resources for industrialized countries. Many of these people live at the minimum subsistence level. They seem to be necessary for people in industrialized countries to maintain or expand their supply levels with the help of low resource prices.

- Limits

Before all, the first thing to consider is that the production of goods cannot be increased infinitely as natural resources are limited.

Environmental protection, the use of renewable energy and recycling can only stretch the supply of resources, but not increase it to infinity. The limited nature applies specifically to the resource environment.

F 6   Impacting the efficiency limits of the real economy driver "Innovative products"

Human curiosity can be said to be natural. It manifests itself, for example, when children want to understand something - to form a concept of something. Children are then sometimes in contradiction with older people who, in a real economy characterized by rationalization, want to take advantage of time-saving routinization and accordingly take less time for children. When children later as adults pursue lingering curiosity, they sometimes think about a business idea.

The realization of innovative business ideas often requires money. Investments in innovations are definitely associated with risk. The profitability of investments in product development is shown by the extent to which the resulting innovative products find buyers. The capital invested is consequently referred to as risk capital. If one part of the investment is not successful enough, another part must yield even higher returns so that the investment sum yields enough money on the bottom line.

Spreading out research, development, production and market penetration over time would make it possible to manage and better calculate the investment risk for innovative products.

The increasing penetration of research, development, production and organization with information technologies is leading to ever faster product cycles. If you want to exploit potential market opportunities for a business idea under these conditions, you are in a race with possible competitors. Accordingly, it is necessary to invest high risk capital in a short period of time in order to be able to realize innovative projects in the shortest possible time. This prevents a competitor with a similar product from entering the market faster and siphoning off the profits. This restriction has consequences for the realization of innovative projects.

- In times of sufficient quantitative real economic growth with a high rate of production and good profits, there is relatively much money and time available for developing new products and projects. The requirements that products and projects demand can be adequately recorded and documented. With sufficient growth in the real economy, there is no pressure to cut required times and prices too tightly.

- If the quantitative real economy weakens, prices for product developments and projects often have to be calculated according to the specifications of the demand market. This often means a reduction in profits and income for the planners, the organizers, the performers and the manufacturers.

- Limits
If the need for innovative products is considered high in order to counter the decline in real economic growth through innovative purchasing incentives, then the need for venture capital is correspondingly high. These funds can be provided by the public sector, banks or private investors.

Particular attention should be paid to the temptation to rely on suggested and presumed illusory returns on investments, which are an expression of high risk. Where the use of venture capital is not rewarded by profitable innovative products, the risk of the capital invested unfolds. The money might disappear without any return for investors.

Insofar as money invested as venture capital is later to serve, for example, the investors' retirement provision, it can leave a gap in provision for the investors' future if the investment fails. These considerations make it recommendable to use savings as risk capital only to a limited extent and in a well-calculated manner.

F 7 Impacting the efficiency limits of the real economy driver „Status gain"

When people become unemployed or have to make do with rather decreasing wages and salaries, purchasing power is lost. Then growth gains are available to a decreasing extent.

Some people with high incomes tend to claim a relatively large share for themselves in the distribution of shrinking growth gains, even if this leaves little growth income for people with low incomes.

Relatively high income increases are, among other things, a consequence of a fusion of interests between employees and employers for the purpose of securing mutual benefits. A fusion of interests with employers is evident, among others, with people living in stable, relatively well-paid jobs. Their demands in collective bargaining regarding participation in growth gains are mostly formulated in percentages. People with high absolute incomes then receive a higher amount as a supplement than people with low incomes. The percentage demands are apparently not unwillingly met by employers, since employees with high income supplements are obviously able to exert a relevant influence on the stability of society as opinion multipliers. They can help keep the disadvantaged, who achieve low growth, at bay.

People with high incomes and the resulting wealth are predestined to buy status goods and thus drive quantitative real-economy growth. Initially, this could compensate for small increases in other people's incomes.

- Limits

However, the increases in income do not only flow into the acqui-sition of status goods, they are also saved. Thus, there is a po-tential weakening of real economic cycles.

People with rather low incomes, whose purchasing power tends to decline, also weaken the real economic cycles. Low-income people would quickly spend more money to meet their basic needs and boost real economic cycles if they did not receive small supplements due to proportional income increases.

The desired stimulation of real economic growth requires, among other things, a more equal distribution of income increases in-stead of proportional income increases. So, people with low in-comes would get extra money and would be very likely to spend it. With equal distribution, higher earners could withdraw less money from the real economic cycle by saving. However, such developments are probably hardly realizable against the will of the high-income and powerful opinion groups in society.

Progressively weakening quantitative real-economy growth po-tentially weakens satisfaction with the state and democracy. It is important to consider and take into account the possible conse-quences.

F 8 Impacting the efficiency limits of the real economy drivers: Environmental protection, use of renewable energy and recycling

On the one hand, it seems likely that with increased purchase of quantitative goods, the use of resources in the form of raw mate-rials, energy and the environment will also increase. It is true that technological progress reduces the resources required for a func-tional unit during its production. However, the increasing amount of purchased functional units and the technical progress with additional new products lead to an absolute increase in the use of resources.

On the other hand, the supply of resources is manifestly limited. Thus, quantitative real-economy growth is ultimately restricted and therefore requires sustainable economic activity. Measures are therefore required to secure the long-term availability of resources such as raw materials, energy and the environment. This means that resources, depending on their type, may only be used to the extent that ...
- they are available for the required time
- they can grow back quickly enough
- they are available as renewable energy. The renewable forms of energy must also replace the non-renewable forms of energy that have been used up to now
- how they remain available with the help of environmental protection
- as they can be provided repeatedly on a considerable scale with the help of recycling.

This group of requirements using resources must be integrated into real economic considerations.

The higher costs of longer-term, i.e. sustainable, resource use - incorporating recycling, renewable energies and environmental protection - are often set against the lower short-term costs incurred without the use of recycling, renewable energies and environmental protection. The more expensive long-term sustainability is subordinated to short-term real economic benefits, so that too many of the resources needed in the future are consumed prematurely.

Price as a regulator of demand to secure the supply of resources probably comes too late. Market activities geared towards the longer-term availability of resources are obviously not present to a sufficient extent.

As a corrective, recycling, renewable energy and environmental protection could be sufficiently supported by state subsidies on the resource market. However, these activities are too constrained by the limited possibilities of the state and the obvious lack of will on the part of the population.

The state can also enact laws that require polluters of waste and pollution to pay the costs of recycling and environmental protection or to cease polluting.

How does the development continue if the consumption of resources continues to increase too much with obviously not infinitely available supplies, if this fact is taken into consideration and if the sum of the individual people nevertheless does not take any substantially effective countermeasures?

-       The individual acting
The individual behaviors combine to form social life. This also includes the real economy.

Within a desire-fulfilling real economy - in terms of desires for quantitative goods and money - it is by definition necessary that there is quantitative real economic growth and that growth gains can be distributed. The increase in quantitative goods for the satisfaction of desires also entails an increase in the demand for resources, knowing full well that their supplies are ultimately limited.

Satisfying desires for survival, comfort and status is the common factor for many individuals. As soon as these desires are transformed into offers of goods and purchasing behavior, the resource stock reacts with reduction.

-       The societal consequences of the sum of individual
        behavior
The consequences of the scarcity of the consumable environment in particular, but also of some raw materials, affect almost all members of societal life in the various countries, cultures and

continents. If the consequences mean an existential threat for almost all people, the behavior of individuals who intensively consume resources and pollute the environment should actually change significantly. Therefore, it seems to make sense to consider the actions of many individuals oriented towards permanent growth gain in connection with the subsequent consequences of their actions for the community.

If in the real economy of a country, with a permanent increase in quantitative goods, the desires for growth gains of all participants can be satisfied, it is comprehensible if the individual participants want to maintain the system that is successful for them.

It is significant that the fulfilment of desires through continuous growth gains only occurs for a part of humanity, but that resources such as the environment and raw materials in particular are reduced to a threatening extent for the whole of humanity.

For the privileged, it does not seem difficult to live with the limitedness of resources. It might seem tempting for them to enjoy the benefits of a contented, stable and democratic society characterized by growth gains. Moreover, it is easy to be unaware of the potential limitations of quantitative real-economy growth due to limited resources for oneself, as long as one is not directly affected by the impact of the limitations. The individual dilemma in the form of the discrepancy between the existence and the perception of resource shortage seems worth highlighting.

F 8.1 Resolving individual dilemmas by forming opinion pools

Social life is characterized by two essential components. On the one hand, there is cooperation, which mainly concerns the exchange of qualitative goods. On the other hand, there is competition, which essentially organizes the acquisition of quantitative goods. The interplay of qualitative and quantitative goods and the prioritization of quantitative goods have already been dealt with. The preference for quantitative goods is also leading to increasing competition between people.

A society organizes both technical and real economic progress and thus the supply of goods largely through competition. This requires strategic thinking, behavior and action.

In times of sufficient quantitative real-economy growth, competition leads to a good supply of qualitative and quantitative goods.

Whereas in times of insufficient quantitative real-economy growth, the distribution of growth gains under competitive conditions can lead to social polarization between those who benefit and those who are disadvantaged.

In a strategic competition-driven environment, it can obviously not be expected that the growth-oriented members of a society limit their competitive behavior in such an effective way as to result in relevant saving of resources. This saving of resources would after all require that the drive for obtaining growth gains was appropriately restricted. The limit of using resources would no longer be determined by competition. The limit of resource use is then determined by the sum of the restrictions to be set individually. If one group submits to a restriction on resource use and another does not, the second group might additionally perceive the benefits of the first group.

The members of a society who are supposed to change their competitive behavior in the direction of saving resources can easily find statements that allow them to set the limits of resource consumption in such a way that they hardly have to cut back.

The statements do not have to be invented by the individual, because they are the result of a discussion that seems to develop by itself in such a way that interested people can rally around the statements that are beneficial to them as a group.

Obviously, argumentation patterns of interest groups automatically assemble in such a way that they can present their advantages as justified. As long as the advantaged are in the majority in a society compared to the disadvantaged, they can logically also significantly influence the formation of opinion in their interest by representing opinions favorable to them. In the following, interest-based argumentation patterns are presented in order to improve the transparency of majority building.

F 8.2   Different group interests

What matters is: - which countries can obtain and pay for resources that are not unlimited - where is waste stored and recycled and who bears the costs incurred - who carries out the necessary environmental protection and who pays for the measures. In the following, we will consider various distributional interests.

If companies from high-wage countries have production carried out in low-wage countries for cost reasons, the corresponding part of the resource consumption initially passes to the account of the producing countries. Furthermore, the costs for waste storage, recycling and environmental protection are also located there for the time being.

The final question of interest is to which of the countries involved the resource consumption and the costs for waste storage, recycling and environmental protection will be attributed. This could be the country that places the manufacturing order, the country where manufacturing takes place, or the country where consumption takes place. Thus, it seems necessary to regulate the distribution mode of scarce resources such as raw materials, energy and environment, including the costs of waste storage, recycling and environmental protection. In addition, who receives the benefit of the use of resources is of critical importance.

In order to determine for each country the amount of allowed use of scarce resources, including the costs to be borne for waste storage, recycling and environmental protection, there are different ways of allocation.

- Percentage increase in the use of resources
The preservation of scarce resources could be defined in such a way that globally all people are entitled to an increase of the same percentage.

-- This determination appears desirable for countries that are at a high average level of resource use per inhabitant. Countries such as these achieve a relatively high amount of increase in deployment authorization using the percentage calculation of the increase in resource requirement. The people of these countries are tempted to help the percentage calculation of the allowed increase of the resource claim to the majority in order to be able to continue to use existing advantages of their growth society extensively.

-- Countries with low average resource use per inhabitant achieve a comparatively low amount of increase in the percentage of permitted resource use. The possibility of real economic development and achieving greater prosperity is thus rather limited for the people in such countries. This could reinforce the emergence of countries that are too underdeveloped in real economic terms and barely organized democratically. There is then the danger that state stability will be established by military means as a substitute because the real economic and democratic foundation is too weak.

- Equal rates of increase in resource use

Rights to resources could be set in a way that equal growth rates per person apply worldwide.

-- This approach seems to be desirable for countries that are at a low average per person of resource use. These countries achieve a relatively high amount of increase in resource use allowance for equal amounts of increase in resource entitlement. The people of these countries are tempted to help this calculation of allowable increases in resource use to become the majority, thus allowing greater real economic growth rates for their societies.

-- Countries with high average resource use per citizen achieve a relatively small amount of increase in resource use allowances if the amount of increase in allowable resource use is globally the same per person. Thus, the possibility of achieving greater prosperity is very limited for people in these countries. This could lead to increasing resistance to such a distribution mode.

- Limits

Due to the different interests of the countries involved, the possibilities for global regulation of resource use are apparently very limited. This also shows the limits of using the means of resource provision to achieve global quantitative real economic growth, equitable distribution of growth outcomes for all stakeholders, satisfaction of all stakeholders, stability in all states, and global environmental protection.

Alternatively, market-driven polarization can be allowed. However, we then have to accept the resulting social and global tensions and their discharges. Foreclosures between countries are likely to be made to ward them off. The latter then apply more to refugees from poor countries, but probably less in the opposite direction when realizing current account surpluses.

F 8.3   Interests - over the course of time

The use of resources and the resulting consequences are sometimes separated in time. This particularly concerns the correlation between resource use and environmental damage. The time aspect is noticeable in two ways.

- On the one hand, some doubt whether the environmental consequences discussed will even occur at a later point in time as resource consumption increases. Beyond the shield of accepted doubt, the current generation can take advantage of the growth society, provided it lives in an advantaged region of the world.

- On the other hand, the generation responsible for the doubts may no longer be alive when the connection between cause and effect of resource use becomes visible. The development may then be so far advanced that its consequences are unstoppable and can no longer be prevented.

There seems to be an interest in exploiting the benefits of growth even if it leads to a consumption of the environment as a resource that threatens the existence of the planet. This behavior is embedded in the apparent ability not to perceive correlations. In addition, many people benefit from the foreseeable limited nature of their lives, so that only later generations are confronted with the consequences of current behavior.

Future generations might ask the following questions:
- **Why did you let this happen?**
- **Why didn't you do anything about it?**

Hopefully, the consequences of the irreversible consumption of resources will not occur abruptly, but will first show themselves with harbingers. However, it is also possible for negative consequences to snowball.

F 9 Impacting the efficiency limits of the real economy driver „Investments"

The distribution of investments by a central authority does not seem appropriate, as such an institution is too similar in its functioning to a centrally planned economy, which has proven its inability to control.

A thought experiment is carried out below. Subsequently, it would be recommended that, in order to prevent the weakening of the quantitative real economy, productivity should be increased with the help of investments, but only to the extent that there would be no unemployment, no overproduction and no resource bottlenecks. If one part A of the companies adheres to these recommendations and another part B does not, then part B could try to force part A out of the market with a larger investment volume and with profitability advantages, in order to determine market events with less competition and more price sovereignty without regard to the above recommendations.

A further consideration shows that there are parallel aspects of investment activities. If, for example, new technologies appear to be necessary on a large scale for reasons such as environmental protection, investment in such new technologies is required. At the same time, the old technologies must be supported financially in the transition phase.

Two transitions can be mentioned as examples: that from coal mining to the automotive industry with combustion engines and its transition to electromobility.

Market activity has so far obviously not led to an optimal allocation of investments in the necessary real economic, technological and environmental transitions. The question arises about the financing of the transitions.

The support of funding for transitions has its limits. Due to ecologically caused strong demand, rising prices and increasing inflation, savers can lose money that should be used to secure the future. Renouncing collective bargaining in favor of the technological future means anticipatory renunciation by today's workers as a contribution to future-oriented investments. The above effects create different burdens for parts of the population.

Securing a sustainable future by investing in technologies that make sense in real economic, technological and ecological terms can also be assigned to the state as a joint task. Then on the one hand, the direct control of success by the market is missing. On the other hand, the market has caused resources such as the environment to be consumed under competitive conditions in a way that threatens the existence of the economy.

F 10   Impacting the efficiency limits of the real economy driver „Education"

Education can be can be divided into two parts. First of all, there is purpose-free education. It is assumed that it is free from other interests of commercialization. Thinking, education and research take place take place for their own sake.

Beyond that, there is purpose-bound education, training education, training, teaching and research. These are oriented, for example, towards individual social, technical or even real economic goals. Results often come about by accident, of course.

A society could for example be described by the exchange of qualitative and quantitative goods, the consumption of resources and by sufficient or insufficient quantitative real economic growth. The development of a society is influenced by education. The following observations show such influences.

- Education and the human enhancement factor

Education is used, among other things, to enable a human enhancement factor using resources such as raw materials, energy and the environment in interaction with machinery and information technology. With its help, a person can produce increasingly more goods in a unit of time. This requires an increasing amount of resources such as energy, raw materials and the environment.

- Education, the human enhancement factor and sufficient quantitative real economy growth

Education helps to create technical progress. It can improve the human enhancement factor. This makes it possible to realize increasing goods output, bring in additional labor and promote quantitative real economic growth on a sufficient scale.

- Education, the human enhancement factor, deficient quantitative real economy growth and social polarization

The human enhancement factor, which increases through education, can not only improve but also weaken quantitative real economic growth. This is shown when, over time, automation and rationalization on the one hand reduce the number of workers needed and on the other hand the quantity of goods produced nevertheless increases. Increasingly more people with lower incomes are then faced with a potentially increasing supply of goods. This means that real economic cycles and real economic growth are beginning to weaken.

Furthermore, polarizing effects on the real economy may become apparent. They are characterized by the fact that, on the one hand, there are increasingly people who earn little due to automation and rationalization, weakening purchasing power and the real economy. At the same time, a grouping of people is emerging that is needed for automation and rationalization, for example, and earns well but also saves, thus weakening real economic cycles and real economic growth.

Education as a part of technical progress, automation and rationalization can thus have a weakening effect on the real economy over time and at the same time drive societal polarization.

- Education leads to relief from heavy physical work, but also to work compression

Education supports technological progress. With its help, heavy physical work can be transferred from people to machinery. Physical wear of people can be reduced as a result.

Rather, technical progress over time leads to a burdensome densification of work, which is supported by information technologies. This happens because organizational and technical processes can be carried out in ever shorter periods of time. The process gaps - caused by coordination and organization that cannot be planned in advance - are becoming smaller and rarer. This means that people can increasingly be made redundant with the help of information technology. Where the elimination of human labor has not yet taken place, people increasingly have to orient themselves according to predefined goals, times and cycles and increasingly divide their time for this purpose.

Furthermore, with the help of information technology, permanent pressure can be exerted to shorten the deployment cycles of the money invested. This means that the associated production, project and innovation cycles are also becoming shorter. Technical progress makes it possible, with the help of information technology, to condense the performance of work to the limits of endurance, so that a burn-out syndrome can develop. It arises, for example, when the compression of work with the help of technical progress leaves hardly any time to breathe and increasingly demands tension and strain with corresponding effects on health.

- Education and change in income

Sufficient quantitative real economy growth is characterized by an increasing demand for human labor, enabling the production of more and more goods through physical and mental labor in interaction with the machines used. As long as there is enough demand for it, a good income is granted.

As time passes, it becomes apparent that the interaction of the real economy, education, technical progress, machinery, information technology, automation and rationalization can partially generate unemployment and income reduction.

- Education and equal opportunities

In times of sufficient quantitative real economy growth, qualified people are urgently needed for production, research and teaching purposes enable further growth with the help of technical progress. They should be able to achieve the required qualifications through education and training. On the one hand, there are people available for these purposes who, in addition to the intellectual potential, also have the financial means to pay for the training. To meet the demand for qualified people that arises over and above this, qualifications are made possible for people who have the intellectual potential but lack the money to pay for the training. This happens under the keyword of equal opportunities. They should be established between the people who can pay for their education themselves and those who cannot and therefore need public support.

When quantitative real economy growth slows down or turns into insufficient quantitative real growth, the focus remains on achieving equal opportunities through education in order not to fall behind in the race for new markets with the help of technological progress.

- Professionals and academics move countries

Trained professionals and academics can be recruited from abroad if there is a need to be met in the recruiting country. These people leave their home countries, for example, because they are not needed there in a bad real economy or because they only earn low incomes there. The training expenses then burden at

least partially the training countries. Extensive migration of edu-
cated people from poorer countries and their immigration to richer
industrialized countries can drive an interstate global polarization.

-    Limits of education, qualification and technical progress
--   Taking advantage of opportunities to participate in growth
  successes with the help of qualification must be viewed in a
  differentiated manner. On the one hand, a lack of willingness to take advantage of opportunities is frivolously assumed. On the other hand, the technology users may also
  be unwilling to provide the time necessary for people to gain
  the qualifications.

--   Education is a condition for technical progress. Technical
  progress needs qualified people who support technology-
  based quantitative real economic growth. The qualification
  requirements often change so quickly that people are sometimes unable to meet them, perhaps due to prolonged unemployment, age or too much stress.

--   Education does not only make it possible to produce machinery with the help of technical progress, to use labor for
  its production and to enable the fulfilment of desires with the
  resulting purchasing power. But education-supported information technology also renders some people unemployed
  or low-income earners over time.

--   Technical progress not only serves to satisfy human needs
  and fulfil desires for goods. It also serves the interests of
  people who want to use it to earn more money and build up
  wealth through the application of automation and rationalization, so that they can in turn use it for rationalization. From
  a certain stage of this development, a new social polarization occurs: on the one hand, people become unemployed
  or earn less due to rationalization, and on the other hand,
  people accumulate wealth and increase the effects of rationalization.

In conclusion, education has different influences on technical progress.

Education acts as a driving force for technical progress, which can, in turn, promote quantitative real economic growth. This can be used to realize wishes in terms of survival and comfort, for example. Education apparently serves the interests of many people.

If sufficient quantitative real economy growth turns with the help of technological progress into deficient quantitative real economy growth, societal polarization can arise. It seems important to look at this polarization later in the context of how it can be influenced by education.

F 11   Impacting the efficiency limits of the real economy drivers "Savings and loans"

If bad real economic times are suspected for the future, consumers are tempted to save as a preventative measure. In this way, real economic cycles can be weakened. If bad times in the real economy are looming or even feared, savings tend to intensify them or perhaps even cause them in the first place. This process is a case of self-fulfilling suspicion.

The government's obvious approach to counteracting such developments is to preventively strengthen the real economic cycles through financial injections. Payments made in this context may go to consumers. They shall spend the money they receive and thus drive real economic cycles. However, financial injections can also be made available, among other things, for companies to develop new technologies and products to be bought by people with corresponding cash reserves, thus strengthening the real economy.

- Limits

In times of still sufficient quantitative real economy growth, the state can take the money deemed necessary for the financial injections from the real economy cycles.

If real economic cycles are weakening, the state will not want to withdraw money needed for financial injections from the richer people, who causally withhold it from the real economic cycles by saving. The state would probably not want to lose the goodwill of these people by withdrawing money they have saved in order to redirect it into real economic cycles for the purpose of driving them.

For the state, it is then obvious to take out the money needed for the financial injections as a loan, i.e. to run up public debt. Usually, interest must be paid on the loans. The repayments of loans, including interest, weaken future real economic growth and provoke new additional loans and interest, the shadows of which can become longer and longer in the rush to repay.

F 12 Impacting the efficiency limits of the real economy driver "Redistribution"

The state redistributes funds in such a way that it withdraws money from the real economy in order to have it available for the fulfilment of common state tasks. This money is given, for example, to people who are disadvantaged or disabled and therefore cannot participate sufficiently in the real economy cycles. Further examples of state community tasks are the responsibility for internal and external security. The money is usually used for tasks that the state can do better than if individuals had to do them themselves on a pro rata basis.

As long as there is sufficient quantitative growth in the real economy and the redistributed money flows quickly back into the real economy after redistribution, tasks that serve the general public are fulfilled without quantitative growth in the real economy being decisively inhibited.

If quantitative real economy growth no longer provides sufficient growth returns for the state to carry out community tasks to the satisfaction of the members of society, the state is tempted to take up missing funds as loans. Alternatively, the state could take the money it lacks for community tasks away from the people who have so much of it that they do not currently spend the available money. But rich people also have strong social influence. If the state deprives these people of increasingly necessary money for the purpose of completing community tasks, it may lose their support. To avoid this, the state is tempted to take out loans.

-       Limits
Loans taken out for the purpose of carrying out community tasks must be repaid, including the necessary interest. The repayments will again weaken the completion of community tasks in the future and make new loans necessary. This shows that public debt for the purpose of carrying out community tasks is in a race with its own ever-lengthening shadow in the form of the required repayments, which at first glance cannot be won.

Therefore, the state obviously tries to get rid of the problem of public debt with the help of low costs for loans and adjusted inflation.

F 13   Summary: Impacting the efficiency limits of the real economy drivers

In case of permanent sufficient quantitative real economy growth, almost all members of a society can, by definition, participate in existing growth gains to a sufficient extent. To be satisfied with the growth gains, it is probably important that the amounts for the different participants are not too far apart and that all participants can have the hope of climbing the ladder of success a little further and a little further. A phase of self-sustaining and sustained quantitative real economy growth as the basis for a satisfied, stable and democratic society can reach its limits when the real economy drivers weaken. These limits can be imagined as follows.

If there is sufficient quantitative growth in the real economy, then desired quantitative goods, the required labor, earnings, purchasing power, consumption, profits and investment increase permanently. All parties involved are continuously confirmed in their expectation that this development will continue.

When moving into the situation of insufficient quantitative real economy growth, the real economy is for example losing purchasing power. This happens in two ways. Firstly, one group tends to earn decreasing amounts of money. This is a polarizing process. Secondly, one group saves its money. At the same time, there is a lack of stimulation of the declining realization of purchasing power through a redistribution of financial resources from the saving of one group to the provision for the consumption and investment mode of other groups.

Societal polarization is appearing as an accompaniment to the transition from sufficient to insufficient quantitative real economic growth. This polarization holds social explosive power between individuals, groups, societies and countries.

In this context, it becomes necessary to consider how societal polarization can be effectively reduced by using as few central "adjusting screws" as possible.

G   **Some ideas for limiting polarization in order to secure not only social and public stability but also democracy**

Polarization in a society is characterized, among other things, by the fact that there are people who ...
- have remunerated work and those who have no work,
- have high-paid jobs and those who have low-paid jobs,
- have higher incomes and those who have lower incomes,
- have fortunes and those who have no fortunes,
- have large fortunes and those who have small fortunes.

Societal polarization is visible between people and population groups.

Societal polarization can arise in the transition from sufficient quantitative real economy growth to insufficient quantitative real economy growth.

With sufficient quantitative real economy growth, almost all people in a society have the opportunity to afford comfort or perhaps even status symbols by sharing in growth gains beyond survival.

The interplay of automation and rationalization can lead to unemployment and declining wages, especially among population groups with inadequate qualifications. This can reduce their purchasing power. As a result, quantitative real economy growth may weaken.

Increasing growth gains and purchasing power, on the other hand, continue to be available for the people who are specifically needed for automation and rationalization. As experience shows, income increases can also be achieved at the expense of other people and population groups.

Some people can earn good incomes and also save their money, others rather do without. This can lead to societal polarization between people and population groups.

Disadvantaged people can become hopeless if they no longer believe that they can keep up with the real economic development. People, population groups or entire countries can be the starting point for destabilizing developments through such programmed discontent.

Societal polarization could be mitigated as follows: A sufficient part of the savings of people with high incomes would have to be redistributed in such a way that it would quickly be recirculated in the real economy. In order to avoid the scarcity of resources, one could try to plan the demand for resources by planning the demand for goods. He money for consumption. The people supported in this way are those who might otherwise play a losing game as a result of societal polarization. Obviously, there is not enough redistribution of savings or even too little income growth distributed equally rather than pro-rata to effectively limit societal polarization.

Looking further, an additional variant of polarization appears, which is the one between two points in time. It reveals itself when real economy growth is accompanied by the consumption of resources, especially the consumption of the available environment. This resource environment risks to decrease in a life-threatening way. This happens between the times when there is initially enough and later too little of the resource environment.

Basically, it seems important to reduce the drive for societal polarization in the area of income. Furthermore, the resource reserve - especially that of the resource environment - should not be reduced in a life-threatening way. In the real economy, market-based self-regulation should be ensured to the greatest possible extent, and no authoritarian rule or central state planning should be established - a planning that, by the way, has proven its inability to work.

The corresponding considerations focus on a few key areas:
- Future-proof handling of resources, in particular the resource environment
- Securing sufficient and well-paid jobs
- Profitability of investments
- Reducing societal polarization through income management
- Redistribution and its alternatives to fulfil governmental tasks

G 1 Future-proof handling of resources, in particular the resource environment

The safeguarding of resources for the future knows several variants, e.g.:
- Planning of the resource demand by planning of the goods market.
- Resource saving technologies
- Environmental protection and recycling
- Sustainable real economy

G 1.1 Planning the demand of resources by planning the market of goods.

In order to avoid the scarcity of resources, one could try to plan the demand for resources by planning the demand for goods. However, as experience shows, people do not base their demand realizations on real-economic goods demand planning of the society of which they are a part. Thus, logically, the planning of resource requirements also fails. Due to this fact, whole economic empires have already failed on themselves.

G 1.2   Resources saving technologies

The increase in the consumption of quantitative goods in the context of permanent quantitative real economy growth brings with it an increasing demand for resources and thus ultimately their scarcity, because their reserves are usually not infinite. In order to be able to counteract the resource shortage, thoughts about a resource use which helps to secure sufficient resource supply for the future are urgent.

The wish for a future-oriented use of resources would have to be supported by the will of self-preservation of a real economic system, which builds on the permanent increase of wish fulfillment by quantitative goods and thus also permanently possible provision of resources, in order to be able to realize desired growth gains. The wish for a future-oriented use of resources would have to be supported by the will of self-preservation of a real economic system, which builds on the permanent increase of wish fulfillment by quantitative goods and thus also permanently possible provision of resources, in order to be able to realize desired growth gains. All people should be able to profit from these growth gains, so that they can be satisfied and agree with their state, and therefore want to guarantee it as guarantor of their real economy.

For the purpose of realizing future orientation, technologies can be used to save resources. This enables more effective use of resources so that they are available for a larger number of goods or for a longer period of time. The extent to which resources can be stretched depends on the willingness to implement such stretching measures early enough and to a sufficient extent for later generations and for poor countries.

G 1.3   Protection of the environment and recycling

If the demand for resources is controlled by the goods market, it will increase until there is a scarcity of resources, which will lead to price increases for goods and thus to an increasing absorption of purchasing power, so that demand for goods and consumption of resources should, according to a first assumption, decrease.

Especially in the case of the resource environment, limits of its consumption are easily exceeded. This can happen if the consumption of the resource environment is delayed too much and leads to consumption-regulating price increases for goods. The too long-lasting consumption of the resource environment can bring global existential dangers.

At first sight, an ideal idea is to stretch the supply of resources by extensive recycling or comprehensive environmental protection. However, the necessary measures are often more expensive than the consumption of existing resources without re-cycling and environmental protection. So the question arises about the acceptance, the realization and above all the payment of effective recycling respectively environmental protection.

Everyone could choose products with sufficient recycling and environmental protection. He would thus be choosing between short-term advantage-taking when recycling and environmental protection levels are too low and long-term resource protection. The transition from short-term oriented to long-term oriented and thus sustainable behavior is obviously only insufficiently accomplished by the sum of individuals.

G 1.4   Sustainable real economy

In a market-oriented real economy, competition among market participants influences whether they succeed in selling or acquiring goods. Decisive for the success of the participants in this competition is their performance. In most cases, performance is oriented on time and prices.

In other words, if a company manufactures a product in the shortest possible time and delivers it at the lowest possible price, it has competitive advantages and is more likely to be successful than its competitors - it has a greater chance of securing its existence and of expanding.

Orientation on time means that continuously higher performances of work and production should be achieved. Thus, more purchasing power can be acquired and real economy cycles can be stimulated.

During a time-oriented development, resources can become scarcer and more expensive. This can affect the prices of goods and reduce their sales. Resources then are weakening as real economy drivers. If resource scarcity causes a weakening of the time oriented real economy, we need to think about alternatives to resource scarcity and time orientation.

-      Resource oriented targets as an alternative to time
orientation
Resources do not only consist of the resource "environment", but also of the two main groups "energy" and "raw materials". Both energy and raw materials are often transported to places of low-cost production in order to bring the products afterwards to customers who pay maximum prices. The transport routes look like a network. They are based on the affordability of raw materials, energy supplies and labor and on the capital strength of the buyers' market. Transport and production are time oriented. The transports mostly take place using energy that is harmful to the

environment. This results in a global polarization between the countries involved.

In this context, the question arises of a more sustainable orientation compared to a primary orientation to time. The answer to this question could be resource orientation. In our first thoughts about resource orientation, we consider whether the production of goods could be positioned where energy is available at low cost in an ecological regenerative form. Additional reflections on resource orientation deal with optimal recycling opportunities to recover raw materials. Finally, we will examine the possibilities and limits of resource-oriented acting.

- Renewable energy as a part of resource-oriented acting.
-- In a first approach to "resource orientation", it seems reasonable to transport raw materials to where energy is available in the form of cheap renewable energy throughout a longer period of the year.
-- Energy-intensive production could take place there to a large extent and at low costs due to the availability of renewable energy.
-- Replacing non-renewable energy with renewable energy serves to protect the environment.

- The second step of resource-oriented acting consists in combining renewable energy and recycling.

As using renewable energy in a growth-oriented real economy continues to promote raw material scarcity, recycling of raw materials is pushing itself into consideration as a complement to the use of renewable energy. The recycling of raw materials is the second pillar of resource orientation, along with the use of renewable energy.

Recycling is becoming more attractive in middle-wage countries compared to high-wage countries. Products to be recycled would be taken to the countries with medium wage levels which were

oriented on renewable energy. These countries then would receive significant raw material shares from recycling in addition to
low-cost renewable energy.

--   Wage costs in middle-wage countries should be signifi-
      cantly higher than in low-wage countries, but significantly
      lower than in high-wage countries. The level of wage costs
      should be seen in the context of production and the recy-
      cling to be coupled with it. Recycling is bundled with the use
      of renewable energies and the production of new goods.

-    Potentials of resource-oriented activities
First, the central question is whether there are potentials for investments in resource-oriented acting. This kind of investment in
a production that is essentially based on renewable energy and
recycling and takes place in countries with medium wage levels
could be made by

--   people from developed countries with savings. Instead of
      investing in purely speculative financial markets, they could
      place their money in a resource-based real economy at a
      reasonable interest rate. When calculating such an interest
      rate, it must be taken into account that the losses of specu-
      latively invested money can be avoided.

--   companies taking action before overusing the environment
      to gain a start-up advantage over traditional companies.
      Switching to renewable energy and recycling would reduce
      environmental and raw material consumption.

The potentials of a real economy oriented towards renewable energy and recycling can be summarized as follows. First, there
would be an increase in the use of renewable energy and recycling in the eligible countries. Secondly, in such countries, avoid-
able losses in the value of speculatively invested money could be
used in the real economy. In the future, money that is no longer
used speculatively could be the focal point of a real economy oriented towards renewable energies and recycling. In the following,

we will show how countries with such a real economy can achieve democratic stability.

- Concentrating on resource centering can set real economy cycles in motion.

If resource-centering is implemented, higher wages would have to be paid in the previous low-wage countries. In these countries, people with increased purchasing power could then buy quantitative goods. In this way, real-economy cycles could be formed. These countries could then become socially stable and democratically organized states and secure trading partners for the traditional industrialized countries. Refugee flows could be reduced. As so-called lighthouse countries, these countries can inspire other countries to follow a similar path.

- Distribution of growth gains in case of resource-oriented action

Regarding the described focus on renewable energies and recycling, it seems reasonable to distribute the resulting growth gains not primarily according to a percentage key, but to a significant extent according to the key of equal distribution. Thus, the drifting apart of income and wealth could be limited. In this way, less money would be withdrawn from the real economic cycles through savings and their weakening would be prevented.

- Limits of renewable energy production and recycling
-- Renewable energy systems must be replaced at the end of their service life. Their production also requires raw materials. Finally, there is also the question of the availability of sites for renewable energy plants if they are to meet the necessary, ultimately unlimited energy demand as the real economy grows.
-- Furthermore, not all appliances, products and goods can be fully recycled at present. This fact must already be taken into account in the planning and design of equipment, products and goods.
- Summarized statements

It was outlined how countries would have to orient themselves in terms of resource targeting in the real economy.

-- They would have to focus on renewable energy
-- Their labor costs would have to be at a medium level. This means that they should be much higher than in low-wage countries but also much lower than in traditional industrialized countries. The level of wages has to be seen in the interaction of the costs of production and recycling.
-- Income increases should rather be equally distributed.
-- In order to build up real economy cycles, money should be available with credit costs based on adjusted interest rates.

Renewable energy and recycling in middle-wage countries could help secure their future by building sustainable industries there.

In high-wage industrialized countries, we know about the amount of labor costs incurred in these countries. In a first theoretical approach to the recycling of products, we can assume that the same effort would be required for recycling as for the manufacture of the products. Hence, a resulting higher cost level of products would presumably be at the expense of the supply level in industrialized countries, since recycling costs would have to be added to the prices of bulk goods and thus people's purchasing power would only be sufficient to buy bulk goods.

The focus on renewable energy as well as on recycling in combination with a medium wage level can offer an alternative to the primarily time-centered real economy in high-wage industrial countries. Recycling is more profitable, at least in part, under conditions of developing real economy countries than under conditions in high-wage industrialized countries. The scope of conflicts can be described as follows.

High-wage countries are characterized by increasing polarization in their countries and in their relationship with poor countries. polarization involves poor people and poor countries being limited in the acquisition of goods and related resource consumption.

Due to this limitation, richer people and countries benefit to a maximum from the remaining resource stock.

Poorer countries would have the chance to create the basis for a sustainable real economy through maximum use of renewable energy and extraction of raw materials through recycling. Wage levels would have to be much higher than in lowest-wage countries but much lower than in highest-wage countries. The formation of a medium wage level is based on the costs of renewable energy production, the costs of recycling and the costs of producing goods. It is possible that the goods markets will then be divided under sustainability aspects into high-wage countries and countries with medium wage levels. This raises the exciting question of functional coalitions that can limit the development of global polarization with its existential consequences.

G 2   Ensuring sufficient employment and appropriately remunerated jobs

To begin with, a brief overview is given on this topic:
- Automation and rationalization and their influence on the number of labor forces required
- Momentum of the labor market
- Strategy ensuring sufficient employment and appropriately remunerated jobs

G 2.1   Automation and rationalization and their influence on the number of required labor forces

Automation and rationalization initially enable quantitative real economy growth. As time goes by, they could weaken it again. The following section shows how this turnaround will take place.

At the beginning of a sufficiently growing quantitative real economy, the interests in, on the one hand, increasing consumption and correspondingly sufficiently paid work and, on the other hand, increasing the production of goods are served in parallel by automation and rationalization. Growth is possible because an increasing number of workers are needed to realize increasing production of goods as well as to support automation and rationalization. Workers earn more and more money and can acquire additional quantitative goods in return.

The purpose of automation is to make work processes as automated as possible and thus to replace labor with machinery, energy and information technology.

Rationalization should ensure that the money spent on automation yields a return.

Along with this development, the increase in automatically produced consumer and investment goods rises faster than the demand for goods at a certain point in time. The result is a tendency towards market saturation. Some labor forces from the production of goods and investment resources are freed up.

As a result, some incomes tend to become smaller because there is an oversupply of workers and they have to be willing to work for less money in the competition for jobs. Some workers do not get new jobs, they remain unemployed and depend on state support. As some workers have to be satisfied with decreasing incomes, their purchasing power decreases. They can buy less quantitative goods.

Tendencies towards overproduction, partly lower-paid labor and a reduction in purchasing power are promoting the weakening of the real economic driver of adequately paid work. This raises the question of how the labor market should react.

G 2.2   Momentum of the labor market

The labor market seems to have an inherent logic in which employment changes by itself.

At first there is the phenomenon of employment increasing by itself in phases of sufficient quantitative growth in the real economy, in which all those involved assume and can assume that wages, salaries, profits, consumer goods and investment goods will increase sufficiently step by step.

Secondly, there is the phenomenon of employment declining by itself, characterized, among other things, by too low incomes and purchasing power, which weaken real economic cycles.

To illustrate this phenomenon, two aspects of the labor market will be examined below. First, there is the lack of self-recovery forces that could lead in the direction of sufficient employment, income and purchasing power. Secondly, apparently independent developments towards insufficient employment are considered.

-      Lack of self-recovery forces of the labor market
Similar to the assumption in the market economy that supply and demand will level off, this is probably also how it is thought behind the scenes in the labor market. This would require real economic self-recovery forces capable to develop the labor market towards an increasing demand for employees with good earning potential as a reaction to its weakening, in order to move it towards increasing consumption and investment and thus sufficient quantitative real economic growth. This could be pushed by the real economy driver "demand for goods".
--   The demand for quantitative goods is unlikely to be met for a long time because of many people's desire for survival and some comfort.

-- The potential demand for quantitative goods could be met with the help of additional employed people, automation and rationalization.

-- The money needed for investment in automation and rationalization could, for example, be provided by the people needed to automate and rationalize the real economy and industry. These people benefit because they have good incomes and can therefore save to invest in automation and rationalization.

However, considering the above, the labor market is not yet moving in the direction of more employment. Obviously, there is no money for those people who would like to fulfill their wishes by acquiring goods and who could thus make employment possible.

Labor markets are apparently not moving enough towards higher incomes and purchasing power for low earners and therefore not towards sufficient demand for goods and therefore not towards a sufficient number of employees. This is partly due to the fact that over time, with increasing automation and rationalization, growth gains are distributed asymmetrically disadvantaging lower earners.

In the real economy, the money that low-income earners lack is not available to buy goods and thus also to maintain quantitative real economy growth. This growth would be a prerequisite for almost everyone involved to receive sufficient growth gains.

Money, on the other hand, is held by people who have saved it and want to invest it in quantitative real economy growth, although investment is not necessarily due to the weakening demand for goods. This situation can be illustrated as follows:

There are two parallel paths.
One path contains goods for markets that tend to be saturated. This saturation is the result of insufficient income and therefore insufficient demand for goods.

2024-05-26

On the other path is money that has been saved for profitable use for investments, but is needed there to a decreasing extent due to insufficient demand for goods.

The money saved is partly lacking those people with too little income. They could use this money to buy goods in future. This would trigger additional quantitative real economy growth, which would then again require saved money for investments in order to be able to produce an increasing amount of demanded goods.

There is obviously a missing link between the two paths described, through which enough saved money can enter the consumptive part of the real economic cycles to drive quantitative real economy growth.

A preventive solution would be to redirect more money into consumption and less into savings accounts when distributing growth gains. This could be achieved by distributing income more equally and less as a proportion. However, such a development has not emerged sufficiently.

-       The independent development of the labor market
As there is obviously no automatic countermeasure towards sufficient income for a part of the population whose income is tending to fall and whose purchasing power is weakening, companies might take the proactive approach. They could raise the prices of their products in favor of higher minimum wages so that they could pay the higher minimum wages in order to create higher purchasing power and trigger quantitative real economy growth. If a few companies act in this way, they must expect to be forced out of the market by other companies that do not pay higher wages and are instead more competitive on the goods market with lower prices than the companies with better-paid labor.

- Summary

As automation and rationalization increase and demand for certain workers decreases, the incentive to pay them sufficiently decreases. Lower-paid work leads to weaker purchasing power and thus to weaker growth in the quantitative real economy.

In this apparently inevitable market situation, people with too little income could simply be left to themselves.

However, this behavior is apparently not fully accepted in the labor market. This is because when looking beyond the borders, we have to realize that against the background of a purely market-oriented logic of income distribution and the distribution of goods, some of the world's people are starving. Thus, there is probably at least a limited interest in approaches to counteract inadequate quantitative real economy growth and to guarantee sufficiently paid work with the aim of an at least partially satisfied and stable society. This is where further discussions on strategies against a weakening real economy should start.

G 2.3 A strategy to ensure sufficient employment and appropriately remunerated jobs

Creating quantitative real economic growth appears to be one way of enabling additional employment. In this context, we will first identify two obstacles and then present the instrument of redistribution.

- First obstacle: lack of money to buy goods
In real economy cycles, money is needed to buy goods. If, for example, people become unemployed or earn too little money due to automation and rationalization, or if people in very poor countries have hardly any opportunities to earn money, then these people cannot generate the necessary purchasing power

to satisfy their needs, pay for their wishes and thus drive quantitative real economy growth.

- Second obstacle: money is taken away from consumption through saving

In addition to people with too little income, there are people who are needed for the real economy, which is oriented towards automation and rationalization, among other things, and who earn good incomes. They can satisfy their survival, comfort and status needs without having to spend all the money they earn on the purchase of quantitative goods. A portion of the money acquired can thus be withdrawn from the real economy cycles through saving and is thus missing as an engine for quantitative real economy growth.

- Redistribution of saved money to increase insufficient income and create jobs

First of all, it should be noted that the purchasing power of a part of the population often tends to fall.

Secondly, other population groups are saving more, thus limiting their ability to realize purchasing power.

Thirdly, for competitive reasons, individual companies are unable to effectively implement the development towards higher wages and salaries for low earners in the real economy. This is an obstacle to the creation of purchasing power.

As a result, it is likely that a state redistribution of money from people with savings towards poorer population groups would be effective for growth, because these poorer people would quickly cover their needs with the money received. The additional needs would then require additional labor forces.

There should be no dispute about redistribution by the state if it serves to provide for those members of society who are unable to participate sufficiently in the real economy due to disability.

Furthermore, the government must be able to use redistribution to fulfill common tasks such as internal and external security, which individual citizens cannot effectively realize to the required extent.

In addition to the typical common public tasks, the government is often called upon to become redistributive in terms of growth.

Money taken from higher earners and wealthy people could be put back into real economy cycles through financial injections - such as transfer payments and subsidies.

If this money reaches the people who quickly feed it back into real economy cycles to satisfy their needs, quantitative real economic growth is boosted and everyone involved can benefit because there are new growth gains to distribute, which can stimulate the demand for goods and the labor market.

Growth-oriented redistribution by the government runs the risk of leaving too little money for investment due to the redistribution towards consumption. The necessary limitations must be taken into account.

G 3   Profitability of invested money

There are various stages of development in the real economy.

-      From manual labor to a complex real economy
If goods are only produced by the human body using energy, no machinery is required and no external energy is needed apart from the energy of the human body. At this level of production, the supply of goods to people would be very limited. However, under such circumstances, if people produced everything they needed themselves, no exchange would be necessary.

If single people only produce special goods, they can multiply their supply through mutual exchange.

If people want to exchange in larger contexts, the use of money for the purpose of simple inter-storage makes sense.

If people want to exchange in larger contexts, the use of money for the purpose of simple inter-storage makes sense.

By using money, machinery, energy, automation and information technology, the purely human use of energy can be multiplied. In this way, an increasing and diverse supply of people with goods is possible.

- From supplying goods to securing the future through saving
On the one hand, many people want to earn more and more money using their labor with the help of machines, energy, automation and information technology and create purchasing power to buy more goods. At the same time, they often want to save money for the future in order to be able to make larger purchases later on or to secure their financial future.

- From saving to investing in quantitative real economy growth
If you only want to use the money you have saved to buy goods later, you can use it to earn additional money in the meantime. The money saved can be made available to banks or companies. Banks lend the money to consumers or companies. Companies invest the money from banks or direct investors in machines, energy, automation or information technology in order to be able to produce the quantities of goods desired by potential buyers.

As long as the money saved is invested in machines, energy, automation or information technology and the additional goods produced with their help are purchased, the use of the money saved serves quantitative real economic growth. Everyone involved can achieve growth gains. The money saved and invested can flow back to the savers, including the returns generated.

G 3.1   Investments in quantitative growth of the real economy can lead to its stagnation

Savings and money used by companies for machinery, energy, automation, information technology and rationalization can result in overproduction and a tendency towards saturation of goods markets. This results in unemployment, declining incomes and decreasing purchasing power for some people. This inhibits quantitative real economy growth. Saved money can then no longer be used to the expected extent to fulfil the return expectations of savers who want to invest the money they have saved. In a continuation of this idea, it would make sense to invest money in technical progress.

G 3.2   Uncertainties of investments in technical progress

Technical progress is the result of research and development. It produces innovative products, new manufacturing processes, automation and rationalization.

New products partially replace existing products. However, they also offer new additional purchasing incentives.

Investment in technical progress often enables processes that make life easier, increase individual safety and save energy and raw materials. These variants of technical progress are often emphasized.

On the other hand, investments in automation and rationalization lead to overproduction, partial wage erosion, declining demand for goods and a weakening quantitative real economy once a certain level of productivity is reached. These variants of technical progress are often underexposed.

Investments in technical progress also influence development in barely industrialized countries. Creating a real economy in these countries through automation and rationalization often prevents the creation of labor-intensive jobs that could generate income and thus real economy cycles.

At the same time, however, global communication and thus access to affluent societies are promoted in these countries. These societies then have to build high walls against people who want to move from countries with an impaired real economy to affluent societies.

G 3.3   Market-driven investment in technical progress

If technical progress is to be application-orientated, it would make sense to primarily let the market decide on the activities of investors with regard to technical progress. Thus, investors must be convinced of the potential success of a product idea and they must weigh up their investment risk against the expected return. This is why public investments in technological progress are recommended to be viewed more critically.

G 4   Reducing societal polarization by adjusting incomes

Increases in incomes for individual people are often calculated as a proportional matter of course. However, as an alternative, it would make sense for income types such as wages and salaries to be increased by a significant proportion of the same amount for individual people and only to a lesser extent as a proportion.

When comparing the increases in income, the proportional shares of the increases are dominant compared to the shares of the same amount. At the same time, it is obvious that powerful people usually receive relatively high incomes. These people receive higher proportional increases in their income than people with lower incomes. It therefore follows that people with higher incomes are in favor of proportional increases and that this type of increase seems to happen for granted as a result of the influence of people with higher incomes.

At a certain level, people with higher incomes will no longer use a part of their income for the current purchase of goods. They can save money in order to be able to make larger purchases later or to secure their future.

In the meantime, saved money is often made available to banks or companies until it is spent. They can use it to finance investments in production facilities, for example, in order to produce the quantitative goods demanded by a growing market.

People with higher incomes who invest their savings in a growing real economy receive a return on the money they invest. Higher incomes are therefore rewarded with a return in addition to the benefits of percentage increases. This further widens the gap between higher incomes and lower incomes.

As long as higher incomes, including the returns received on them, and lower incomes as a whole flow back into the real economy cycles as quickly as possible for the purpose of acquiring goods in the consumption sector and investing in the production sector, jobs and purchasing power are created and quantitative real economy growth is stimulated. In this phase, almost all people involved in real economy cycles receive growth gains in the form of higher wages, salaries, profits, redistribution by the government and in the form of more goods.

Even if incomes increasingly diverge with proportional increases and partially additive returns, there are hardly any acceptance problems as long as all people share in the growth gains and people with lower incomes at least feel they have the chance to move up the income ladder.

Money from people with prosperous incomes is often invested in the manufacturing sector, where it develops an automating and rationalizing character. In this process, human labor is replaced by machinery, energy and information technology and the volume of goods produced increases.

As soon as the quantity of goods produced in the consumer and investment sectors increases faster than their demand, this results in overproduction, unemployment and a reduction in income and purchasing power. Quantitative growth is thus inhibited. It will then no longer be possible to serve the interest in generating returns through investments in automation and regionalization as usual. As soon as automation and rationalization cause overproduction and tend to saturate goods markets, thus promoting unemployment and lower incomes, the generation of growth gains decreases. There are two groups of people involved in the real economy.

On the one hand, these are the people whose incomes continue to rise because they are needed in the real economy, which is characterized by automation and rationalization. This is particularly the case because companies are in a competitive race for survival, which they want to secure through rationalization.

On the other hand, these are people who become unemployed or whose incomes tend to fall because, for example, there are too few job offers for their qualifications.

G 4.1 The splitting into groups with prospering and weakening incomes

We combine people with higher and still rising incomes into one group and call them the group with prosperous incomes. They can still participate in growth successes.

People with decreasing incomes tend to be characterized by inadequate or unneeded qualifications, unemployment or dependence on state support and can hardly participate in growth successes. We group these people together in the low-income group.

The following describes how the separation of the population into groups of people with prosperous incomes and those with lower incomes appears to be happening by itself.

In times of sufficient quantitative real economy growth, almost everyone involved can produce and participate in growth gains with the help of automation and rationalization and thus realize his or her own satisfaction. This development is driven by the actions of all those involved. Low-income earners do this primarily through their satisfactorily rising income and increasing consumption. Other people, with prosperous incomes and savings opportunities, do this not only through consumption but also by investing in a prosperous real economy, receiving a return on their investment.

Over some time, a gradual process of overproduction, a tendency towards market saturation and a partial reduction in employment and income can set in, which is also driven by automation and rationalization. This development can then be the cause of the division into groups that continue to prosper and those that are tending to lose income.

However, it is not easy to identify the cause of the divergence between prosperous and low incomes at first glance. This is because both prosperous quantitative real economic growth and satisfactory incomes for almost everyone involved and, subsequently, weakening quantitative real economic growth and the emergence of low incomes for part of the population have the same causes. These are automation and rationalization.

In the context of the same causes, the transition from sufficient to weakening quantitative real economy growth is becoming more and more blurred. This also makes it difficult to recognize the transition from a good income for almost everyone to a division of society into groups with prosperous and poor incomes. The blurring transition makes it impossible to clearly assign the causes of high and low incomes.

G 4.2 The apparent personal responsibility for belonging to an income group

On the one hand, people with higher incomes like to portray themselves as being successful and attribute their success to their own performance, although their disproportionately increasing incomes are often the result of the proportional distribution of growth gains.

On the other hand, people are easily declared to be personally responsible for their unemployment and low incomes.

These two income groups deserve to be examined in more detail.

G 4.2.1 To be recognized for belonging to the higher income group

In times of sufficient quantitative real economy growth, people with higher incomes participate more than sufficiently in growth successes. Furthermore, they also have enough time to acquire and exchange quality goods such as free help and cooperation. The conditions for mutual recognition in the group with higher incomes therefore seem to be fulfilled. In times of insufficient quantitative real economy growth, the group with higher incomes is confronted with a special challenge. In competition with their equals, they have to spend more and more time to achieve their higher incomes. Since the time required to achieve high incomes is increasing, there is less time left for the exchange of qualitative goods such as unpaid interaction as part of the social community. This is how you can suffer from gaining recognition.

G 4.2.2 Losing hope due to belonging to the low-income group

In times of sufficient quantitative real economy growth, there is nevertheless sufficient participation in growth gains for the low-income group. There is also enough time for these people to exchange quality goods, such as free cooperation.

In times of insufficient quantitative real economy growth, people whose incomes tend to be too low often have fewer opportunities to adapt to qualification requirements and therefore have diminishingly justified expectations and hopes regarding sufficient or even increasing participation in growth. People with weakening incomes are more likely to see their purchasing power decline. Therefore, we can understand when these people accept the given circumstances as unchangeable and their hope turns into a loss of hope. Missing purchasing power can possibly be alleviated by mutual unpaid help.

G 4.3   People and their affiliation to income groups

On the one hand, there are groups of people with higher incomes who are successful for a variety of reasons.

On the other hand, some groups of people are less successful in the real economy because, for example, they have no or poorly paid work due to disability, a lack of or unneeded qualifications or a lack of resilience.

Some groups are presented below:

- Groups of people with individually enforceable higher incomes
-- These are, firstly, qualified people whose scarcity allows them to push through higher incomes These people are needed for research, development, automation and organization, among other things.
-- These are people in positions of power who may have high incomes to defend. In times of increasingly rapid technological change, however, such positions of power are also at risk if the success that these people are expected to achieve fails to materialize in the face of increasing competition in the real economy.
  And there are also people who can use large fortunes like in a game to win enough games and be successful on the bottom line.

- The group of people who can collectively increase their income
These are, for example, trade union members. They are rewarded for their membership by being part of a powerful community of interests that can help shape collective agreements concluded between employees and employers. Trade unions and their members are an easily calculable factor for goods manufacturers when it comes to paying wages and salaries, setting product prices and planning production. So there are interests that

bring employees and employers together and also keep them to-gether.

Trade unions are integrated into the real economy through collective agreements. The improvements agreed therein are largely made on a percentage basis. This means that the income gap is also widening between union members. Members with higher incomes have a special interest in stable cooperation with goods manufacturers in order to be able to underpin their advantages in the form of proportional increases in income. To ensure that the widening income gap does not lead to dissatisfaction among people with lower incomes, non-percentage increases are sometimes made, e.g. to compensate for interim conditions without collective agreements.

If some quantitative goods can no longer be produced profitably enough in a country due to increases in wages and salaries, e.g. in order to meet the expected return on savings of people with higher incomes, the production of such products is consequently relocated to countries with lower income levels. After transitional periods to cool down agitated tempers, unemployment also materializes for union members. People who become unemployed are obviously no longer of great interest to the trade unions.

Unions seem to have to keep organizing activities like strikes to attract new members. They can thus protect themselves financially in the event of strikes.

Too little increase in small incomes could be compensated for by distributing growth gains evenly rather than as a proportion. This would give the word "solidarity" an updated gloss for trade union members, because people with lower incomes would be able to buy more quantitative goods with the help of the resulting higher income increases for them.

The strategy of much more equal distribution of growth gains would bring decisive improvements for many people. The conditions for a more stable society would also be established because more people would be able to participate sufficiently in growth gains.

- Groups of people with low incomes who are characterized, among other things, by disability, a lack of or unneeded qualifications or a lack of resilience.

In times of sufficient quantitative real economy growth and not too advanced automation, these people can almost entirely be in sufficiently paid working conditions.

As automation and rationalization increase, the use of machines, energy and information technology will make some people redundant as job holders. This often concerns jobs that require fewer qualifications and are therefore relatively easy to automate.

Technological development is enabling increasingly complex automation using information technology, which is producing new technological generations at ever shorter intervals. Accordingly, the demands on the employees still required in terms of qualifications, effectiveness and flexibility are becoming increasingly greater.

The more the skills of automated production and organization increase, the more people with good qualifications can be replaced. As automation becomes increasingly efficient, people who are disabled, who lack qualifications, who no longer have the qualifications they need or who are not resilient enough are needed less and less. Among them, the number of people becoming unemployed is increasing. This means they are more likely to get lower-paid jobs or remain unemployed. These people mainly make up the low-income group.

People with low incomes, wages and salaries or with income from state transfer payments often weaken the real economy over time. These people will hardly be able to act as real economic drivers. They, in particular, benefit compensatory from cheap quantitative goods that are produced in low-wage countries.

The group of beneficiaries in the context of societal polarization

Insufficient money supply for people with low incomes could be supplemented at the expense of people who receive a higher share of the growth gains from the real economy and save a part of it. Consequently, money would be redistributed from savers with relatively high incomes towards people with too low incomes, who could quickly return it to the real economy cycles to meet their current needs. This would drive quantitative real economy growth and enable new rounds of distribution of growth gains to all participants.

People with good incomes obviously refuse to accept what they perceive as excessive redistribution.

Over time, people with low incomes simply accept their situation by receiving a financial minimum from the state and settling in accordingly. When people with low incomes have given up hope of being able to enter prosperous real economy cycles with adequate incomes, the splitting of the population into those with good incomes and those with low incomes stabilizes.

In particular, people with a good income can easily claim in defense of their own situation that people with a low income are satisfied with their situation and apparently do not want to change it. They, on the other hand, can present themselves as those who have acquired good and necessary qualifications and who have the necessary physical and mental resilience and therefore earn good incomes.

However, a significant group of people with good incomes are those who, through skillful representation of their interests, have secured their vested interests in times of economic prosperity.

168   2024-05-26

The vested rights and their protection were established, for example, through legislation as well as through the defense of group interests such as trade unions. These vested rights are a basis for taking advantage in the course of social development. In a changed economic situation with weakening real economic growth, the beneficiaries would like to continue claiming their entitlements from the time of a comprehensively prosperous economy on the basis of the established vested rights. They also do this at the expense of people with low incomes, e.g. through the proportional distribution of growth gains.

But how would the situation be for vested rights holders if they could not rely on vested rights that they had established for themselves in times of economic prosperity and instead had to organize their current working life under competitive conditions, as is the case for many other people?

New answers to this question are likely to emerge as soon as the group of vested interests loses political weight as a result of demographic developments.

G 4.4   Countries with relatively rich or relatively poor populations

Similar to the societal polarization in industrialized countries between people with higher and lower incomes, there is a global polarization between rich industrialized countries and poor countries that have hardly any industry of their own.

On the one hand, it can be observed that hardly any industrialized countries are building up money-generating industries on their own. These countries rely, for example, on people who have emigrated and been trained as skilled workers in other countries and who then return to build a bridge between the industrialized and developing countries.

However, it can also be observed that poor countries lack the money to implement state structures, state security and a minimal healthcare system.

Industrialized countries have the potential to promote positive change for poor countries. But changes tend to happen in favor of industrialized countries that try to benefit from poorer countries in competition with each other.

The interests of industrialized countries in poor countries can be seen in the form of:
- sourcing raw materials as cheaply as possible
- selling expensive industrial products
- headhunting of skilled workers
- subsidizing own agricultural products with the help of industrially earned money to establish own agricultural competitiveness vis-à-vis less industrialized countries. This makes their agricultural export more difficult.

In this context, it seems important for industrialized countries to have stable structures to ensure beneficial economic relations with poorer countries. The connections to the poorer countries obviously involve the influential people there. They may establish stability in their countries, which is also guaranteed with the help of authoritarian leadership. To derive alternative approaches, we must take a closer look at the current account differences between countries. The states are characterized by different histories and development. Consequently, different countries are also characterized by different real economic situations. Some tend to have a current account surplus and others tend to have a current account deficit.

As long as the current account surplus does not become too large and does not lead to payment difficulties on the side of the current account deficit, there is a rather tension-free situation in which balanced mutual real economy action can be possible.

As long as the current account deficit does not become too large and does not lead to payment shortfalls on the side of the current account surplus, a rather tension-free situation with a promising future is also possible here, which allows mutual action on an equal footing.

Tension-free situations should be used to prevent possible tensions in the future. On the current account surplus side, this concerns tensions in the population resulting from payment shortfalls, falling exports and declining employment. On the side of the current account shortfall, these are tensions in the population if the reduction of the shortfall causes financial shortfalls and worsens the supply situation.

Reducing tensions between countries with very divergent current account balances would require balancing current account surpluses and shortfalls.

This could be done by making it easier for countries with a deficit to export more goods at reasonable wage levels and prices.

However, current account balances are obviously not being balanced to a sufficient extent because countries with current account surpluses would have less growth gains to distribute at home. As a result, their quantitative real economic growth could suffer, as could the acceptance of their politicians by the population.

In a next step, it seems necessary to get to the core of the problem of current account differences.

Non-competitive countries take out loans to cover the costs of their state. These costs arise, for example, from the need to settle a current account deficit if the state has made imports or is liable for imports. The money for the loans is provided by banks from rich countries. When countries become insolvent, they need new loans from richer countries. To this end, the poor countries must undertake to use part of the new loans to repay the old loans plus interest.

Both sides get involved to a certain extent in such interlinked financial transactions.

Competitive countries are doing this to prevent poor countries from going bankrupt and thus also to prevent the loss of money lent to poor countries by banks from richer countries. This behavior arises because the richer countries are partly liable for the banks' loans to poor countries. If loans could not be repaid, the liable states would have to intervene.

The poor countries remain in the role of permanent repayers of loans plus interest. Countries that permanently have to pay interest on current account deficits are also paying for the prosperity of the other side. Such a development can have consequences in poorer countries, such as internal unrest and authoritarian state systems, which may then try to ensure state peace and stability militarily.

Such states may eventually become ungovernable and slide into chaos with consequences that are hard to imagine for the rich industrialized countries.

This means that tensions between rich and poor people can build up, and not only in rich countries. Tensions can also arise between poor and rich countries, which can cause major problems for both sides.

Ultimately, it seems reasonable to reduce the risk of over-indebtedness for poor countries by allowing them to use the threat of national bankruptcy as a warning. In order to reduce the risk of sovereign default, the banks' lenders could ensure that the banks effectively limit over-indebtedness and lending risks when lending to poor countries. The risk of state bankruptcies appears to be a market-compliant instrument against excessive debts.

G 5   Redistribution and alternatives to redistribution to fulfill state tasks

It is an essential task of the state to fulfill its communal duties, such as ensuring internal and external security. However, this also includes care for people with disabilities. These are primarily physically and mentally disabled people who do not earn enough money to live on in order to participate adequately in real economy cycles.

In order to carry out such tasks, the state must redistribute money from the real economy in order to carry out its communal tasks.

In addition, another state task has crept in, namely that of redistribution towards non-disabled people with too little income. The development towards this task is described below.

Saving by people with higher incomes removes money from real economy cycles. The money saved is available for saving targets such as buying a car or a house. Moreover, some people have such high incomes that they have no current savings targets for the purchase of additional goods due to the short and long-term needs they have already met. They may then use the money saved to secure their own future or that of their children.

As long as money saved is not needed for current expenses, it is e.g. available for investments in automation and rationalization. Automation and rationalization mean that after a period of quantitative growth in the real economy, people become unemployed or their incomes fall. Their purchasing power is decreasing, while product manufacturing continues to increase. This leads to a weakening demand for quantitative goods and a tendency towards market saturation due to overproduction.

On the one hand, money is withdrawn from the consumption cycle through saving and, on the other, through a decrease in income. Both phenomena are leading to a decline in purchasing power and demand for quantitative goods.

In this context, the question arises as to what extent demand can be increased and production boosted so that people with falling incomes can work and earn more again.

Considering this, it might be reasonable that the state should take on an additional task on top of its traditional communal tasks by redistributing some of the money stored through savings to people with low incomes, who then quickly would return it to the real economy. This approach would enable a continued real economic growth and the subsequent distribution of growth gains to satisfy all members of the society, and thereby support the stability of the state as a foundation for democracy.

G 5.1   Redistribution - Satisfaction - Stability

The state undertakes redistributions in order to fulfil its communal tasks. The money withdrawn from the real economy for this purpose is used relatively quickly for specific tasks and thus relatively quickly returned to the real economy. In other words, redistribution does not cause any significant stagnation in the real economy. If money is withdrawn from people who save money, this money flows more quickly back into the real economy after redistribution than without redistribution. From a growth-related perspective, what happens when sufficient quantitative real economy growth turns into insufficient quantitative real economy growth?

-      Times of sufficient quantitative real economy growth
Then almost all people in a society can receive increasingly more income and goods. Incomes usually increase proportionately. People with higher incomes thus receive a higher supplement

than people with lower incomes. There is a widening gap between people with higher incomes and those with lower incomes.

As long as quantitative real economy growth provides sufficient growth gains for almost everyone, the divergence of incomes is obviously accepted. People with lower incomes can also hope to move up the income ladder.

As long as the members of a society are satisfied with obtaining quantitative goods and they also have enough time to acquire qualitative goods, the conditions for a stable society are obviously met.

In times when almost all members of a society have sufficient quantitative real economy gains and sufficient time to acquire qualitative goods, the feeling of subjective distributive justice among individual members of society can lead to social satisfaction and state stability.

- Times of insufficient quantitative real economy growth
If automation, rationalization and the asymmetrical distribution of growth gains lead to a tendency towards overproduction and a reduction in purchasing power, sufficient quantitative real economy growth can turn into insufficient quantitative real economy growth. Over time, there may no longer be enough growth gains to allow everyone to participate sufficiently.

Some people become unemployed or their income tends to fall. In addition, proportional distributions of income penalize people with lower incomes. The gap between people with higher and lower incomes is widening.

People on low incomes can feel hopeless if they have little chance of moving up the income ladder.

In times of insufficient quantitative real economy growth, the feeling of living in a socially fair society presumably diminishes among people with lower and declining incomes. This can affect the stability of a society.

If the state wants to counteract such developments, it is tempted to strengthen a weakening real economy by injecting money into it.

Initially, it would seem reasonable to withdraw money from those people who, while earning well, withhold it from the consumption cycle by saving and thus weaken it. If the state quickly returns this money to the poorer people through redistribution and thus indirectly to the real economic cycle, this can be strengthened.

People with higher incomes are probably against such redistribution. This seems reasonable because their perceived recognition through high incomes could be seen as diminished.

If the state wants to prevent the weakening of quantitative real economy growth but does not want to take the money for redistribution from people with higher incomes, it has to resort to borrowing.

In return, people with savings offer their money to the state in order to receive a return. This can be used to replace income from investments in automation and rationalization that are no longer profitable.

The state's borrowing to drive a weakening quantitative real economy leads to national debt. At first glance, this would appear to be an alternative to state redistribution, as the interests of lenders from the high-income group and borrowers from the low-income group appear to be overlapping. The questions of what happens if the real economy continually demands new loans and what role interest rates play remain unanswered.

G 5.2 National debt as an alternative to redistribution by the state

If the state takes out loans to boost a weakening quantitative real economy, it can reduce the direct redistribution from rich to poor people. Using the loans, the government then tries to stop the weakening of the quantitative real economy through financial investments from loan pots and thus get the real economy on a growth path again.

The credit pots are filled partly by those who have withheld money from the consumption cycle by saving, and thus contributed to the stagnation of real economic cycles. As the stagnating real economy requires less saved money for investments in automation and rationalization, savers can pay into state loan pots as an alternative in order to receive returns from there.

On the other side of the credit pot are those interested in receiving money from the state as aid in the form of subsidies and transfer payments. There are, for example:

- Companies that want to develop more effective, environmentally friendly or workload-reducing systems, machinery, equipment and products in order to be able to compete and survive, both nationally and internationally.
- Universities that want to invest in research with government support to invent and develop new products for consumption and manufacturing that can open up new markets.
- Educational institutions that want to raise the qualification level of unemployed people to prepare them for new jobs.
- Unemployed people or those with too little income who would like to be supported.

In other words, offers of aid from the state as subsidies and transfer payments generate creative interested parties. These are competing with each other to receive aid payments.

A new task is added to the state's task of carrying out community tasks, i.e. the implementation of credit-financed aid payments to various social groups. The payments are supposed to help promote quantitative real economy growth.

The groups receiving the money are competing with each other to receive the aid payments. These funds are intended to enable their recipients to participate more effectively in the development of the real economy. Demands on the state seem to be implanted with a justification that is supposed to make the demands undeniable. This works in such a way that demands are justified by the fact that some groups achieve higher growth rates than others. In the logic of this way of thinking, it is considered fair that groups with lower growth gains receive additional money as aid payments from the state, paid for from its borrowing.

State aid payments are intended to drive quantitative real economic growth, prevent or overcome weak growth and bring growth successes for disadvantaged groups so that their demands on the state lose their cause.

Since the fulfillment of wishes usually quickly generates new wishes, fulfilling wishes with the help of aid payments appears initially to be a wonderful way of ensuring permanent quantitative real economy growth.

If the state withdraws money from the real economy in times of sufficient quantitative real economy growth and thus fulfills common tasks, this money usually flows quickly back into the real economy circles. These are unlikely to be weakened by this.

If, in times of insufficient quantitative real economic growth, the state permanently provides the real economy with money in order to boost it and takes out loans for this purpose, part of the money provided is saved in order to make provisions for obviously uncertain financial times.

Furthermore, a part of the credit-financed money, which is intended to drive the real economy circles, must be spent on national credit management.

In many cases, interest has to be paid on the loans that are used to provide the aid payments.

Inflation and the cheapening of the money supply are a good way to counteract government debt and its accompanying consequences.

If the state takes out loans to finance aid payments in order to strengthen the quantitative drive of the real economy, this involves repayment and costs for administration and often also for interest. Furthermore, some of the aid payments received are used for savings. These monetary transfers do not serve the purpose of stimulating real economy growth, but they still must be paid later and thus generate further loans.

Realizing aid payments through national debt is causing an ever-increasing volume of loans. Inflation and the cheapening of the money supply are a way to counteract national debt and its accompanying consequences.

- National debt and inflation

Inflation occurs when, despite an increase in income, the value of the income received does not increase accordingly because prices are rising at the same time.

Inflation can also happen in a different way. If goods become more expensive, people with non-increasing incomes and people with savings can buy less for their money. Over time, these people see the value of their money decline.

We see a polarization between different population groups. On the one hand, there are the people whose incomes rise in line with price increases. Their standard of living remains the same.

On the other hand, there are people whose incomes are not increasing or who live on savings - such people can buy fewer goods when prices rise and the value of their money decreases.

The following section examines the process of the loss of value of money through inflation with regard to the state and its debt. If loans that were taken out by the state for aid payments and that led to national debt only have to be repaid after a longer period of time, the burden on the state as repayer is reduced if inflation occurs in the meantime, because it then only has to repay the same amount for the higher value of the borrowed money at a lower value. By borrowing, however, the state had the opportunity to use the borrowed money with a high value for desired real economy purposes such as boosting quantitative real economy growth in order to pay it back later at a lower value.

But for people who are not receiving increasing state support or who have saved for retirement, inflation means a corresponding loss in the value of their financial income and security.

These people are likely to be the natural opponents of inflation-accompanying national debt. However, they must be aware that the state has an interest in a limited loss of value of the money, because the state then only has to pay back the same amount with a lower value for a higher value of the borrowed money.

The intergenerational contract is a conservative alternative to saving for the future. This means that the generation of pensioners who are no longer working can expect the same pension or support payments as those earned by the generation that is working at the same time. Then savers, for example, have less to fear from the loss in value of their future-securing savings, because as pensioners they can live at the adjusted level of the future generation. But it is precisely the intergenerational contract that has been undermined by various government measures.

We have to think about how the negative consequences of national debt can be mitigated while still generating quantitative real economy growth. The realization of growth successes then serves to enable a satisfied and stable society. For this purpose, it is important to realize the intergenerational contract.

\-   National debt and cheapening of the money supply
In times of weakening quantitative real economy growth and the associated worries about the future, people have an incentive to save more money than they would if there was sufficient growth. However, saving additionally weakens the demand for goods and quantitative real economy growth. There is a phenomenon of self-fulfilling expectations with regard to worries about the future.

If the demand for goods falls as a result of savings, the prices of goods could be lowered in the competition for consumers. In this situation, consumers are tempted to postpone their spending in order to wait for prices to fall further. This will further weaken quantitative real economy growth.

In order to mitigate such a looming downward spiral of real economy development, there is a temptation to make the money supply cheaper. This measure is intended to provide an incentive for people to accept the money on offer and take on private debt - in order to channel the borrowed money into the real economic cycles for the purpose of consumption or investment. These activities are then intended to initiate quantitative real economy growth. If successful, this could reduce the amount of national debt that serves the same purpose.

However, it can be assumed that weakening quantitative real economy growth will limit rather than promote the need for credit for the purchase of consumer goods and capital goods. This limitation is due in particular to debt-limiting worries about the future on the consumer side and excessive production capacity on the manufacturer side.

If the real economy is obviously hardly demanding loans for consumption and investment, the temptation to try to boost the real economy in the traditional way with cheap money is great due to the obvious helplessness. Instead, this money is then used for purely speculative purposes, for example, in order to earn money with money. However, this obviously does little to stimulate quantitative real economy growth. For this reason, it is important to think about alternatives for real economic growth without losing sight of real economic development.

G 5.3   Alternatives to national debt

To begin with, we can state the following: If quantitative real economy growth weakens because, for instance, some people receive too little income as a result of automation and rationalization and other people save money as their income increases, the state could redistribute money from the richer people to the poorer people so that they can consume more and quantitative real economy growth can thus continue.

As richer people would understandably resist redistribution wherever possible, the state is tempted to stimulate the quantitative real economy with the help of national debt. The lenders are those people who save money and invest in growth in times of sufficient quantitative real economic growth. During the transition to inadequate quantitative real economic growth, they can use their money as a substitute for loans in the form of national debt. This should then generate quantitative real economy growth. The loans must be repaid, including the money diverted. The advantage for the state is that the value of government debt is reduced by inflation. At the same time, the value of the money that people have saved to secure their future or that they receive as a low, non-increasing income is also falling.

When the acceptance of growing national debt for the purpose of boosting a weakening quantitative real economy reaches its limits, it is necessary to think further about alternatives to national debt and strengthening the real economy. This will be shown under the following headings:

- National debt and its prohibition
- National tasks and their alternative financing
- Supplementing the real economy with speculation
- Separation of economic cycles into real economic and purely speculative financial cycles
- The time aspect in speculative trading
- Speculation - from the minority opinion to the majority opinion
- Taxation of speculative trading.

5.3.1   National debt and its prohibition

If quantitative real economy growth is weakening and insufficient growth gains can be distributed to meet the expectations of the people involved, measures to counter the weakening of the real economy obviously make sense.

Firstly, there is the possibility of using political decisions to channel saved money that has been withheld from the real economic cycles to poorer people, who then presumably spend it quickly on consumption. This is of course opposed by the owners of the savings and the politicians who want to maintain the goodwill of these people.

The state is then tempted to promote quantitative real economy growth through aid payments by taking out loans and running up national debt. Limits to the effectiveness of government debt have been demonstrated.

Initially, it seems advisable to stop practicing public debt. However, this does not eliminate the causes of the weakening real economy as a trigger for national debt, which are as follows:

- Some people might become unemployed as a result of automation and rationalization. Incomes and purchasing power then tend to fall.
- Saving, preferably made by people with higher incomes, deprives the real economy of money.
- Incomes usually increase proportionately. This means that they are moving in different directions. There are people with increasingly high income. At the same time, there are more and more people with low incomes and low purchasing power.
- At the same time, prices are rising in many areas, which means that people on low incomes in particular can afford less.

If the quantitative real economy weakens due to the above influences and the polarization between rich and poor people increases, social dissatisfaction can develop.

The limits of national debt as an instrument have been shown. If national debt is abolished, the causes of societal polarization will remain. The task remains to strengthen quantitative real economy growth in order to boost the satisfaction of society's members through the distribution of the generated growth gains. It is therefore important to think about instruments that can be implemented as an alternative to national debt.

G 5.3.2   National tasks and alternative ways of financing them

There are tasks whose completion is important for the society, but which cannot simply be accomplished through separate individual activities. These are typical community tasks that the state is at least partially responsible for. This includes, for example, ensuring external and internal security, as well as education and public transportation.

Since driving quantitative growth in the real economy has also crept into the package of joint state tasks and the resulting national debt can thus become increasingly large, the limits of its financial viability are becoming apparent. Subsequently, we consider how government tasks could be financed alternatively.

- In the field of education, private financing is certainly possible. If you do not have the necessary money, you have to forgo the appropriate education. If a society is interested in broadly defined education-based development, the state must at least partially finance education, supplemented by private funding in specifically desired areas of interest.

- In the transportation sector, private road financing is hardly practicable at first glance because road usage fees may be due depending on ownership rights. This applies in particular where the strategic ownership of access routes to important facilities makes it possible to obtain appropriate remuneration for their use.

There is an interesting financing option for the transportation sector. The state acts as the principal builder. The construction management may be left to private companies, provided they work more effectively than the state.

If companies are not only entrusted with construction management, but also with operator management for state facilities, they can calculate a corresponding return on investment. This occurs in the following contexts. Investors include those with relatively high incomes who are able to save. If money saved is withdrawn from the real economy, this can promote the weakening of the real economy. In a weakening real economy, it is no longer easy for investors to generate the returns required. As a result, investors lend money to the state so that the state can finance national debt. If the state is no longer able or willing to continue this, it will try to outsource tasks, for example by handing over related sub-activities such as construction management and operational management in transportation to private entities. These entities can then invest their savings there and thus secure a return.

The repayment of privately invested money and the provision of returns is then the responsibility of future generations. However, they may also have to deal with the consequences of a weakening real economy, which the previous generation may also have left behind.

Now it could be argued that a privately financed transportation system should be part of a competitive economy. But for many places, there is hardly any competition to charge user fees as part of operator management. As soon as a lack of competition invites abuse, the privatization of such investment areas only makes limited sense.

The privatization of state tasks as a measure against stagnating quantitative real economy growth therefore apparently has its limits. Consequently, further consideration must be given to finding alternatives to national debt as a means of stimulating a weakening quantitative real economy.

G 5.3.3 Supplementing the real economy with speculation

First, the functions of money in the real economy are described and then speculation with money is examined.

There are two main groups of goods in the real economy. These are consumer goods and capital goods. Money is needed to sell and buy goods if you do not want to exchange goods for goods. Money can be collected from the sale of goods and money can be used to pay for the purchase of goods. Money serves as a generally valid medium of exchange.

But money is not just a universal medium of exchange. It can also be used for temporary storage, e.g. when goods are sold and other goods are purchased later. Money also has longer-term aspects. You can save it to be able to make larger purchases later. Money can also be granted or taken out as a loan. Loans are usually granted against payment of interest, which must be paid by the borrower. Loans can enable companies to take advantage of market opportunities ahead of time. Consumers can fulfill their wishes ahead of time with a loan.

Money transactions, savings transactions or credit transactions are often carried out by banks. It is their task to carry out actions with money. Banks, for example, operate the interface between private individuals as investors and companies that need money for investments or for the processing of goods transactions. Banks also handle financial matters between private individuals.

In combination with goods, money is an essential component of the real economy. The sale of goods and their payment as well as the purchase of goods and their payment form real economy cycles. These are goods from both the consumer sector and the investment sector. The cycles are interconnected and form a real economy network.

In times of sufficient quantitative real economy growth, almost all people involved can, by definition, receive growth gains generated by the real economy in order to satisfy desires for survival, comfort or status.

Almost everyone involved wants to maintain growth gains on an ongoing basis. This also applies if people with a corresponding income save money and this money is not needed for investments in the real economy when quantitative real economy growth is weakening and if this money is not brought into real economy cycles. The money saved can then still be kept for old-age provision or to secure the future of future generations, but is waiting to be used in the meantime. Consequently, in these cases, money saved is withdrawn from the real economy through savings and weakens it, while almost everyone involved continues to desire growth without generating sufficient growth.

Nevertheless, savers obviously have little interest in the state withdrawing the money they have saved when the real economy is weakening so that it can be quickly returned to the real economy after being redistributed to poorer people, thus enabling further growth for all those involved and combating the weakening of the quantitative real economy.

The redistribution of saved money for the purpose of early consumption and the achievement of growth for everyone involved would mean that the people giving up the money would not be able to save it for their own security and future. They would have to trust that future young generations would act in the same way as they do by channeling their savings into real economy cycles in order to enable growth in the future to provide for the generation that has become old in the meantime.

People who would agree to give up a sufficient amount of saved money in order to realize continuous growth would have to trust that all future people would remain faithful to this principle. According to this logic, those giving money to one generation could expect to benefit from the next generation and its growth gains. This confidence is obviously not sufficiently present. Instead, people with greater savings opportunities are using their opportunities to lend their money to the state so that it can take out loans and run up national debt in order to stimulate a weakening quantitative real economy. When national debt reaches its limits, people with greater savings opportunities will still want to achieve good returns, as is familiar from times of sufficient quantitative growth or high-interest national debt.

These people have a further incentive to earn additional money with money. This seems to be possible in the first instance by realizing speculation.

-        The way to speculate by investing money
When money is used in the real economy for purposes other than consumption, the aim is usually to generate a return. In other words, additional money is to be earned in order to compensate for inflation or to enable additional consumption, investments or savings.

Companies often bring realized profits back into real economic cycles themselves by investing them.

Banks can organize the use of private savers' money by granting loans to companies.

However, people who have saved money privately can also make it available to the companies directly by acquiring shares in them. In return, they can receive dividends and thus participate in growth gains.

Companies become attractive to the various investors by paying the highest possible dividends. This means that they are subject to the constraint of working as profitably as possible in order to generate an attractive return and thus obtain investors' money to invest in their company.

This approach requires, for example, that companies no longer manufacture unprofitable products, close unprofitable parts of the company or outsource unprofitable production to low-wage countries. This development is primarily made possible by increasingly improved information technology. The controlling that can be realized in this way allows an increasingly better allocation of costs to the products and their selection in terms of profitability.

If share certificates are in demand because of the dividends paid, their price rises. As a result, the purchase of shares is influenced not only by the expected dividend, but also by the realized or expected share price development.

But share price developments do not only depend on dividend payments. Share price increases in particular are probably also driven by the frequency with which shares are traded. In this context, shares are often only bought in order to provoke the smallest share price gains. As soon as these occur, shares are sold again as quickly as possible - but are also bought by other market stakeholders. The fast trading of shares always creates the impression of desirability. The perceived desirability can then drive buying incentives again and these can again increase desirability. Such transactions are likely to tempt investors to use their existing money to make new price gains with a certain degree of probability and thus obtain additional money. The payment of returns by the real economy then appears to be of lesser importance.

We may assume that, from a certain point in their development, prices are no longer primarily the result of return expectations based on the real economy. Instead, price movements are probably also the result of a short-term shortage of shares to enable speculative profits.

Apart from the real economy, in which money is needed to buy and sell goods and to save and lend, there also exists a speculative financial sector. In this branch, money is primarily moved for speculative purposes in order to obtain additional money.

Obviously, not only saved money is used for speculative purposes. Loans are also used. This seems particularly reasonable when quantitative real economic growth is weakening. When the interest rates for borrowed money are low, this is intended to incentivize borrowing. The loans are intended to promote consumption, investment, quantitative real economy growth and thus the satisfaction of as many members of the society as possible. In a period of weakening quantitative real economy growth, money offered at low interest rates is more likely to be used for speculative purposes than for real economy purposes. Thus, people try to obtain more additional money with the help of speculation with borrowed money than is required to pay the interest for the borrowing. The procedure consists in triggering purely financial market activity through money movements. A high frequency of money movements simulates scarcity and this creates the impression of desirability and the incentive to buy shares in order to increase their trading value and realize price gains.

In times of a poor quantitative growth in the real economy, when returns are less likely to be achieved by investing money in the real economy or in national debt, there is an incentive to earn money through speculation. In this way, the figures for the amount of money used are to be increased without having to move real economic goods for consumption or investment.

Speculation gains can be realized in particular by people with higher incomes, savings and assets. They can also provide additional securities for borrowing. These people also have the potential to win strategic games in the purely financial sector with the help of the money they can use. Speculation can increase polarization in society.

If a critical number of speculative investors seem convinced that their speculative gains are insufficient, this is probably reflected in their selling shares. Increasing sales of share certificates reduces the impression of share certificate scarcity and causes a fall in their trading price. If the sale value of the share certificates is lower than the purchase value, this means a realized loss in value for the investors.

In summary, it can be seen that a purely real economy can be accompanied by a partially speculative financial economy.

Hence, financial success occurring as returns testifies that the real economy can generate adequate growth gains. The resulting increase in the price of the share certificates is then an expression of the realized yield.

As soon as stock price gains are generated not only on the basis of good yields, but to a large extent with the help of speculative trading, it is increasingly possible that at a certain point the speculative trend may lead to a fall in prices and to losses for the speculating investors. This is the first approach to a limit to long-term and consistent success under profitability aspects in a speculative financial sector.

The impact of purely financial speculation makes it necessary to consider other alternatives for driving quantitative real economy growth in order to use growth gains to increase the satisfaction of the people involved and thus support state stability.

G 5.3.4 Separation of economic cycles into real economic and purely speculative financial cycles

In order to generate speculative success, investors obviously often try to realize only small price gains. This is done by continuously buying and selling company shares. This is presumably intended to create the illusion of the desirability of shares in order to provoke repeated small price increases.

In conjunction with the phenomenon of price increases due to high trading frequency, trading with shares is obviously also accompanied by assumptions, expectations and visions regarding the companies to which the shares belong.

For some people, trading with company shares based on high trading frequency, assumptions, expectations and visions is the content of their speculative activities. These people can be characterized as attaching less importance to sufficient payouts by companies, which would allow them to prove that they can effectively manage the money they receive on a real economy basis. These people are speculating before distributions are made in order to realize capital gains.

If the speculative use of money to achieve share price gains is initially successful, it may not be successful after a certain point in the purely speculative financial development. As soon as people start to have doubts whether they can realize continuous price increases by buying and selling share certificates and these people also feed the doubts of other owners of share certificates by selling them, an avalanche of selling can be triggered. Thus, the illusion regarding the desirability of the shares and their price increase can burst like a bubble.

When the success of speculative trading collapses, some people may have invested money they saved shortly beforehand speculatively in order to achieve capital gains. If the market value then falls dramatically, these company shares can only be sold at a correspondingly lower value if a sale is required. If it subsequently becomes necessary to sell shares, for example to cover cash requirements or because a fall in the share price appears irreversible, a corresponding loss in value will arise. The difference between the purchase value and the sale value is the realized loss in value. Prior to the loss, quantitative goods could have been purchased for these values. If many people become part of these developments, large amounts of speculative money could be destroyed.

In order to prevent the bursting of a financial bubble, many people may try to get their invested money paid out if there are suspected preliminary stages of a financial bubble bursting. If the money in real economy cycles is not separated from speculative money cycles, funds from real economy cycles can also be used for withdrawal in addition to the funds from speculative cycles. People who only use their money in the real economy and not for speculative purposes ought to expect that even their money will be paid out until their bank becomes insolvent. So the money of these people has to stand in for people who want to make new money by speculating with their money. According to this logic, people with primarily real-economy-oriented monetary investments are obviously included as potentially liable parties in the considerations of people who make speculative monetary investments

If banks' liability for money used in the real economy and money used for speculative purposes is not separated, the state may feel obliged to prevent banks from becoming insolvent, even in favor of those who use money for speculative purposes, in order to possibly ensure solvency in the real economy.

For these reasons, banks should be required to separate the liability of money used in the real economy from that used for speculative purposes. The separation should protect people who do not use their money for speculative purposes from the effects of speculative activities. Thus, the state would have no reason to be called upon to rescue banks in order to save the speculative financial sector.

In this context, the interest of speculators in not separating real economic and speculative funds becomes evident.

G 5.3.5   The time aspect in speculative trading

In order to limit the system-damaging effects of financial speculation, time regulations can be incorporated in addition to the separation of real economic and speculative-financial cycles. This can be done by permitting the sale of share certificates only after a fixed period of time after their acquisition. Thus, it is possible to slow down the self-dynamic and avalanche-like emergence of price gains and, in particular, price losses, making them more controllable and more accessible to intervention.

In these contexts, it is important to ensure an appropriate period of prohibition of trading in share certificates between their acquisition and sale. The influence of the trading frequency on price changes should be reduced to the extent that system-destroying rapid price changes are sufficiently limited.

However, it should be considered that short-term speculative success is often achieved with the help of algorithms defined in computer programs. If there is a period when trading in purchased shares is prohibited, the algorithms must logically also be adjusted.

G 5.3.6   Speculation - from the minority opinion to the majority opinion

In addition to the time-limited trading ban, a further period could play a role for speculative financial activities. This is the period in which the social acceptance of financial speculation with its negative effects may decrease and a distance to speculative financial investments may develop. This idea can be explained as follows: In games, there are winners and losers. This also applies to speculative trading on financial markets. There are substantial opportunities to lose. The question arises whether a significant number of speculatively active people might take consequences for their behavior and perhaps even change it.

G 5.3.7   Taxation of speculative trading

Along with the separation of real economy and purely speculative financial cycles or the introduction of a minimum period between the purchase and sale of company shares, the speculative use of money can be influenced by imposing taxes on speculative profits depending on the frequency of trading or the period of ownership.

The taxation of speculative profits could be set up like an adjusting screw by increasing the rate of taxation per thousand with increasing trading frequency or decreasing ownership time in order to reduce the speculative incentive appropriately. The collected taxes can be used as follows:
-    Reducing national debt. In times of low or even negative interest rates for credit-financed national debt, reducing this debt initially appears less attractive. However, as higher interest rates may be possible or even sensible in the future, it is advisable to reduce national debt as a preventive measure.
-    Expenditure on environmental protection. This money could quickly flow back into real economy cycles.
-    Assistance for people whose wages and salaries are too low.
-    Supporting export opportunities for countries with an excessive interest burden due to a current account deficit, as these countries can be a source of international tension.

G 5.4   More equal and less proportional increases in wages and salaries

Wages and salaries are usually increased on a proportional basis. People with higher incomes thus receive a higher supplement than people with lower incomes. The income amounts are diverging.

People with higher wages and salaries are receiving more and more money that they can save, e.g. to buy a car, build a house, build up a pension or secure the start of their children.

Until savers need their money for one of the exemplary purposes, they can make it available for industrial investments, the financing of government debt or speculative investments as required.

However, if income increases were to flow in larger proportions to people with lower wages and salaries, these income shares could quickly be channeled back into the consumption cycle because poorer people have a lot of unfulfilled current desires.

If this allows the real economy to remain permanently on a sufficient growth trajectory, more people will be able to participate in growth gains.

In order to achieve the sustainability of quantitative real economy growth, the necessary increase in wages and salaries would have to take place in the form of equal amounts rather than as a proportional increase.

If we want to limit societal polarization appropriately, the amount of money available for the increase in wages and salaries would have to be distributed equally among those involved. Furthermore, it would probably make sense to enable an appropriate real economy potential for investments through a proportional increase in income.

G 5.5   Taxation of investment income

It hardly seems possible to align a real economy to planned targets. Instead, it should be able to develop largely of its own accord, driven by desires for survival, comfort, status, etc. However, if a societal polarization that has an existentially destructive effect begins to emerge, it is advisable to consider ways of influencing it once a certain degree of polarization has been reached. Ideas are presented for this purpose.

Societal polarization arises at the heart of the market economy, which is competition. Competition is the driving force behind behavior that continuously strives for more quantitative goods, for survival, comfort, status, etc. Automation and rationalization are reinforcing factors for the fulfilment of more and more desires. This development can create different variants of polarization.

- Polarization in the paid work sector

In a first step, automation and rationalization lead to a need for workers for their implementation, who become redundant in the area of the production of consumer goods.

With increasing automation and rationalization, workers are then released who are no longer necessary for the production of consumer goods or for the production of capital goods in the field of automation and rationalization. These employees are often people who no longer fulfil the changed qualification requirements. As their numbers increase, these people are then often only paid low wages or they become unemployed.

On the other hand, the demand for well-paid workers is increasing, provided that these people are qualified to implement automation and rationalization.

- Polarization in the income area

If part of the population tends to receive lower wages or salaries, their purchasing power also tends to fall. However, in between such a part of the population, there is also another part that receives higher incomes and is able to save a part of it, thus at least partially withdrawing it from the realization of purchasing power. Purchasing power tends to weaken and incomes become polarized.

In times of an increasingly weakening real economy, people with higher incomes can often no longer use their money to make worthwhile investments in the real economy. Instead, they can lend it to the state, which can use it to run up national debt in order to possibly maintain or stimulate the faltering quantitative real economy growth.

When the effectiveness of national debt reaches its limits, people with higher incomes also use their money for speculative purposes in order to obtain additional money.

People with relatively high incomes and savings opportunities can increase their incomes with the help of the activities described and the resulting returns, interest or speculative profits, even if the income of other sections of the population decreases in relative terms and quantitative real economy growth weakens. As a result, we can see further polarization in the area of income.

-       Polarization in the financial assets sector
On the one hand, polarization in the real economy creates people with low incomes and few opportunities to accumulate financial assets. On the other hand, there are people with higher incomes who accumulate financial assets and can increase these through interest, returns and speculative gains.

If the growth gains available for distribution are primarily distributed asymmetrically, reinforcing the polarization processes described above, this can be reflected over time in a weakening real economy and declining social satisfaction.

In order to counteract social dissatisfaction in a weakening real economy, money earned through purely speculative financial activities in particular could be taxed.

Taxation should be organized in such a way that people from the non-real economy have to pay a higher contribution for higher speculative profits than people with lower speculative profits.

It is advisable to start taxation at a low level and use it as an adjusting screw to limit the societal polarization driven by financial speculation.

Then, the effect of taxation would have to be observed in order to include it in the considerations on optimal taxation in order to limit societal polarization.

Once collected, the money should be quickly channeled back into the real economy.

H Minimizing the societal or global polarization by corrective quantitative real economic growth and by reducing the consumption of resources – especially the environment

Two central aspects must be brought together. First of all, there is sufficient quantitative real economic growth in order to achieve social and global satisfaction. The second aspect concerns the conservation of resources - especially the environment - to ensure global survival.

It is assumed that people increasingly want to fulfill their desires for survival, comfort and status by receiving growth gains. We need permanent quantitative real economic growth if we wish to continuously distribute growth gains.

We can see that quantitative growth in the real economy is being driven by automation and rationalization. This development leads to social polarization, particularly in combination with the asymmetrical distribution of growth gains. This concerns …
- work - there are people without work and people with work
- income - there are people with low incomes and those with high incomes
- financial assets - there are people without financial assets and those with different amounts of financial assets. Financial assets are created, among other things, by accumulating savings, interest, returns and capital gains.

The emerging societal polarization can be explained, for example, by the fact that some people receive less and less money. As a result, the purchasing power is weakened. Purchasing power is also weakened by rich people saving. Thus, money can be withdrawn from the consumption cycle which are a part of the real economic cycles The real economic cycles can weaken. This can be counteracted by taxation and redistribution.

- Redistribution can take place preventively by increasing wages and salaries significantly by an equal amount. Simultaneously, a proportionally reduced amount of polarization-promoting increases would remain.

- The missing money can be redistributed from the richer people to the poorer people, who are likely to quickly spend the money they receive to promote growth by feeding it back into the real economic cycles, especially the consumption cycle.

- Redistribution can also take place reactively by taxing income, returns, interest or speculative profits. Taxation should also increase as income rises. The redistribution may only reach such an extent that it does not weaken the real economic cycles by withdrawing funds required for investments.

It seems reasonable to increase redistribution and taxation in very small steps in order to be able to regulate the real economic reaction in the form of quantitative real economic growth. This way, the real economy can be influenced at central levers.

The money collected through redistribution and taxation should be distributed to reduce social and global polarization. This includes reducing public debt, strengthening consumption by increasing low incomes and reducing the current account deficit in the countries concerned.

If permanent quantitative real economic growth becomes possible by redistribution, this implies a corresponding increasing demand of energy, raw materials and environment. Therefore, it is important that an increasing real economy becomes sustainable through the use of renewable energy, recycling and environmental protection.

Investments in a sustainable real economy can be made - among others - by the following groups:

- Individuals who do not want to entrust their savings to speculative financial cycles, but who are oriented towards the real economy
- Financial companies that collect savings from people who do not operate in speculative activities
- Insurance companies that have to pay for environmental damage and therefore invest sustainably as a preventive measure
- Companies that collect income from resources such as oil or natural gas and then invest sustainably.

Investments in real economic cycles should therefore be sustainable. These investments are most effective in countries with medium wage levels and high potential for renewable energy. The interaction with profitable recycling, which serves to preserve the environment and safeguard resources, is absolutely essential in this regard. The profitability of recycling is supported by the adjusted average wage level. In this context, it would make sense to integrate the appropriate product manufacture.

Countries offering the use of renewable energy, comprehensive recycling and the associated appropriate product manufacturing at a medium wage level are likely to be confronted with obstructive interests on the part of high-wage industrialized countries.

High-wage industrialized countries allow low-wage countries to produce cheaply, thus indirectly subsidizing them and preserving global polarization. Alongside this development, the money of rich people and rich countries is seldom invested in the real economy of poor countries in a way that would enable a sustainable improvement in prosperity there. As a result, poor countries' ability to consume resources is kept low and resources are available to rich people and rich countries for more years.

Furthermore, the consumption of resources by richer countries must be seen in the context of environmental pollution and damage to the climate and oceans. The consequences of damage to the climate and oceans can rarely be controlled by the richer states in such a way that the poorer states are primarily affected by negative impacts. This is due to the fact that damage to the climate and oceans is primarily spread through the air and water and therefore knows hardly any geographical boundaries. The polarization caused by damage to air and water is an ecological variant. It takes place between two points in time. At time one, there is still enough of the existentially necessary resources of sufficiently good climate and water. Time two is characterized by the fact that a critical time limit has been exceeded with regard to the damage to air and water. This ecological polarization does not occur as a geographically limited variant, but as a global variant. In this variant of polarization, the richer states cannot primarily shift the disadvantages to poorer states, as is possible with polarization into rich and poor states. There, the separation can be achieved by seas, walls and fences.

Two polarization variants have been shown as examples. First, there is polarization driven by the real economy with regard to many resources and quantitative goods. Secondly, there is the ecologically driven polarization with regard to the environment available for use in the form of the climate and water.

It is now necessary to consider ways of limiting the different variants of real-economy and ecologically driven social and global polarization. With this in mind, we will examine information and information technology because of their central role.

I Information - information technology

As already described, it is assumed that the entire human coexistence can be described by qualitative and quantitative goods and their exchange relationships.

Qualitative goods are exchanged. When negotiating the exchange value of many of these goods, the relevant information is exchanged beforehand. Other everyday qualitative goods are simply given and taken without negotiating the exchange value.

Quantitative goods, however, are bought and sold. Their value is expressed as a number. This also includes the corresponding currency. These two details constitute the information on the value of quantitative goods and the currency used to pay for them These two pieces of information are the cornerstones of the quantitative real economy.

Over the years, a further area for using money has established itself besides using it for trading quantitative goods in the real economy. We are talking here about pure speculation. This is where people try to obtain additional money just by using their existing money.

In speculative economics, as in the real economy, the value of money is represented by information expressed in the form of a number and a currency figure. Speculating can be profitable for some and a loss for others. If purely speculative money loses value, the loss of value for using it in the real economy is lost. This process can have serious consequences both for individuals and for the whole of society, especially if the loss of value occurs like an avalanche.

We only briefly touch a discussion about digitally documented and managed currencies in combination with digitally monitored behavior. In authoritarian social systems, this combination could be targeted as a complete digital social organization. It could claim to manage all quantitative and qualitative goods centrally, including polarization. Developments in dictatorial states should give rise to preventive measures to counter the destructive effects of polarization in democratic states in order to underpin the real economy in democratic states as an alternative to dictatorial systems.

Existing social polarization in democratic states leads to considering information and information technology. This is important because money with its information content is embedded in societal polarization with regard to the measurement of the value of goods. Information is considered under the following headings:
- Information in interaction with goods
- Individual information
- Societal information
- Political information
- information technology

I 1   Information in interaction with goods

Information helps to coordinate human cohabitation, that can be represented by the exchange of qualitative and quantitative goods.

Communication sometimes takes place with qualitative goods, where information is given about the exchange value of the goods to be exchanged to enable an agreement to be reached on the exchange. However, not all qualitative goods must be exchanged with communication. Mostly, qualitative goods are simply given and taken. Communication itself is often a qualitative good. Sometimes it even has to be paid as consulting.

With quantitative goods, information is important in several aspects.

2024-05-26

- Information and its confidentiality

As key players in the real economy, entrepreneurs often have a strong interest in keeping information confidential. This applies particularly to strategic areas. In these areas, the aim is often to achieve competitive advantages on the market by maintaining confidentiality. This may enable profits to be increased in order to realize greater quantitative real economic growth than is possible for the competitors.

As long as there is sufficient quantitative real economic growth in the real economy as a whole, some companies are more successful than others, but only a few companies are forced out of the market because most earn enough money to survive.

A weakening quantitative real economy leads to selection between companies. Companies that are better positioned than their competitors in terms of innovative products, technical equipment, organization and strategy have a better chance of survival. Successful confidentiality of information - e.g. in product planning and market strategy - can have a further impact on sales and profits.

- Information defines the value of quantitative goods

Quantitative goods have a specific price, which derives, for example, from production costs, competing offers and customer demand. The buyer can use these as a guide. The prices determine how much and which goods people can purchase according to their own purchasing power in order to ensure their survival or to achieve a certain level of comfort or status.

The information on the value of a good is given as the amount of money required to purchase it in a given currency. In the context of real economic activities, payment is often no longer made using money with notes and coins. Mostly only figures on the corresponding amount of money and its currency are transmitted and settled. These figures represent a type of information in the real economy.

I 2   Individual information

Individuals can gather and process information and draw personal consequences for their behavior. The total of individual decisions, e.g. regarding the acquisition of quantitative goods, determines essentially what happens in the real economy. A picture of the supply of people with quantitative goods emerges from the realized acquisitions of goods.

In times of sufficient quantitative real economy growth, the fulfilled individual desires can easily lead to social satisfaction.

In times of insufficient quantitative real economy growth, there may be more and more people who for reasons such as automation and rationalization, are unable to earn enough money to guarantee their livelihood, while other people benefit from this development. This polarization of income can lead to an increasingly asymmetrical supply of people with quantitative goods. In this context, further reflections on the negative consequences of societal polarization arise.

I 3   Societal information

In times of sufficient quantitative real economy growth, there is by definition enough time for almost all members of a society to earn enough money to buy quantitative goods - and also to acquire the necessary amount of qualitative goods.

If sufficient quantitative real economy growth turns into insufficient quantitative real economy growth, another similar phenomenon becomes apparent for almost all people, namely a decreasing time available for the acquisition of qualitative goods. This concerns not only people with inadequate incomes but also those with good incomes.

In low-income jobs, people have less and less time to acquire qualitative goods because they have to work longer and longer to earn the money needed to acquire quantitative goods.

People with good incomes are often in severe competition with other people with similar incomes. They often have to work very intensively and for long hours in condensed work processes in order to defend their good income in competition with others. Consequently, they also have less time to acquire quality goods.

Both population groups with low incomes and those with good incomes appear to be confronted with the phenomenon of decreasing time to acquire quality goods in a weakening real economy. The one group has to work longer in order to earn a sufficient income, while the other has to work longer in order to keep their job in competition with others.

Both groups are likely to differ in the degree to which their own skills match the skills required. The two groups could come together in a pool of the dissatisfied due to decreasing private time to acquire quality goods.

The decreasing time available to purchase quality goods appears to be relevant for large parts of society. The two groups with good and poor incomes find themselves in a pool of potential dissatisfaction due to the lack of quality goods. However, these groups obviously do not feel they belong together because of this circumstance, because they presumably perceive themselves as being separated from each other by different qualification standards.

Having shown how the time required to acquire quantitative and qualitative goods varies for groups with different incomes, we will now look at the drifting apart of incomes.

- Groups with diverging incomes
The acquisition of quantitative goods allows individuals with good qualifications and a good income, for example, to show that they

can afford comfort or even status symbols. These goods do not only serve their own perception of value. They are often also intended to have an effect on the outside world in order to gain external recognition.

As time passes, differences between people can increase, which can be seen, for example, in different levels of possession of quantitative goods. The differences can increase when sufficiently strong quantitative real economy growth turns into insufficient growth, as will now be explained.

During periods of sufficiently strong quantitative real economy growth, there are sufficient growth gains for almost all members of society. The difference between richer and poorer people remains small enough to be acceptable to poorer people. The poorer people may think it would be possible to receive enough themselves in the distribution of growth gains.

In times of insufficient quantitative real economy growth, the growth successes available for distribution become smaller. One group of people receives more money, the other tends to receive less. One reason for this is that the distribution of growth gains is usually based on proportions. Richer people with higher incomes then receive more bonuses than poorer people. The gap between people with higher and lower incomes is widening.

-    Calling for justice

If the incomes of poorer and richer people diverge greatly, poorer people may raise the idea of justice. Initially, this concept is more individually based. As soon as many poorer people subsequently call on richer people to redistribute their income to the benefit of poorer people in order to realize justice, a demand that embraces all individuals is born. Many poorer people could unite around this idea and make their thoughts on justice socially relevant. Richer people could develop the following counter-strategies

- Confidentiality of wealth and envy-based discussion
Considering the above, it is logical that richer people want to keep their wealth secret so as not to give rise to possible calls for re-distribution.

The alternative to secrecy is an envy-based discussion. It there-fore seems only natural to present personal wealth as the result of personal achievement, even if it is based on speculation, for example. Viewing their own achievements in this light, richer peo-ple can criticize the demand for redistribution by poorer people as unjustified. The demand for redistribution in the name of justice can be dismissed as based on envy. Richer people can bundle their interests with the help of this argumentation.

- Social classes as a consequence of societal polarization
In times of sufficient quantitative real economy growth, the build-ing of social classes and social tensions can be largely prevented by ensuring that all members of the society can participate suffi-ciently in the growth gains.

In times of insufficient quantitative real economy growth, parallel societal polarization can generate groups among which tensions arise. Thus, the question arises of how to reduce societal polari-zation.

I 4   Political information

There is, at first glance, a simple way out of societal polarization. The parties involved can agree to use political instruments to stimulate quantitative growth in the real economy for this purpose.

The money required for quantitative real economy growth and the desired accompanying reduction in social polarization must then be supplied by the state. To this end, the government runs up national debt. The money needed is provided by the people whose money can no longer be used profitably enough for direct investments in a weakening real economy because the latter only needs investments to a decreasing extent. Then the state is ready to pay the desired return on the loans taken out for the purpose of national debt and economic development to the richer people who provide the money.

-        Political promises
Politicians are often tempted to promises that they can influence developments in the real economy, to get elected. In this context, they run up national debt. The loans taken out for this purpose must later be repaid plus any interest and administrative costs. But experience shows that national debt only delays the weakening of a quantitative real economy growth. However, there are limits to guaranteeing quantitative real economy growth permanently with national debt.

-        Disenchantment with politics
This development could possibly lead to disenchantment with politics or even the state among that part of the population which has to repay the loans for the national debt plus any interest and administrative costs They could even get criticized by those who benefited from the national debt by loaning the state their savings made in times of sufficient quantitative growth. This development may weaken the stability of the state and of democracy. The political recipes of national debt obviously cannot permanently solve the problem of societal polarization and its consequences. Therefore, it seems necessary to broaden the focus. To do this, information technology is included in our considerations.

I 5   Information technology

Quantitative real economy growth at an advanced level can be driven further with the help of automation and rationalization, for example. The technologies used can be divided into the following development and application levels.

- Technologies used for the mechanical production of goods controlled by people and for the technical control of machines.

First there is the technology used to produce goods. This technology involves machines whose control was initially reserved for people. The next technological development steps transferred the control of the machines to technical equipment. Their development can be divided into the following steps:

-- Mechanical control
-- Precision mechanical control
-- Electrotechnical control
-- Electronic control
-- Information technology control, consisting of hardware and software

Of course, the development of the control systems did not proceed strictly according to the above list. All these steps are closely interwoven.

- Technological and economical island solutions and their networking

The increasing technological progress is making control systems more and more complex. Machine processes are being automated. Machines can be combined to form ever larger technological systems. The term "machinery" can be used as a collective term for this. Islands of largely automated production can also be docked onto islands controlled according to economic aspects, for example:

-- market analysis
-- product and project development
-- purchasing production materials
-- manufacturing
-- distribution and sales
-- purchasing by the customer

--   interaction between the product and the customer
--   global networking of companies

The aforementioned islands can be networked. Islands and networks can work increasingly autonomously. The humans are left with residual functions, ensuring process safety, troubleshooting, further development and consumption.

During technological development, the term technology is supplemented by the term information. The resulting concept of information technology plays an increasingly key role. In this context, sensor technology is of great importance. Data recorded by it is processed, usually digitized and then made available for use.

The information technology can collect, link and evaluate complex private, technological, economic, military and social data at great speed and then make the results available to the people. Decisions for people are often already pre-structured. Furthermore, decisions are increasingly being made automatically. Processes can run automatically to an ever-greater extent. To this end, information technology works with algorithms that people are given. In this context, the topic of information technology is structured as follows:
    Vulnerability of networking
    Interaction between generations
    Orientation on the labor market
    Supply of goods
    Suppliers and consumers of goods
    Breaking down secrecy
    Orientation aid for refugees

I 5.1   Information technology - vulnerability of networking

As technological development progresses, the networkability of information, information carriers and information processing systems play a central role. In conjunction with technological development, companies, for example, can coordinate their informational activities. They can also try to gain advantages. Obtaining these advantages often takes place in a climate of secrecy and competition. Competition often invites several interested parties to compete for the acquisition of generally accessible information, secret information and advantages. The more complex the informational network becomes, the greater the risk of vulnerability of the network and the risk of defenselessness of some poorer participants.

I 5.2   Information technology – Interaction between generations

The development of technologies has always involved that they required the people to change within the duration of human generations. Information technology, however, creates many significant changes within the period of a human generation.

Before information technology existed, the younger generation depended on the experience of the older generation. Accordingly, there were dependencies and subordinations. As a result, the diffusion of research results into practical application took a relatively long time, as long as the habits of older generations slowed down the application of innovations.

Once information technology became decisive for the processing of information, a dependency in the opposite direction became visible. The younger generation is growing up with the new technologies as a matter of course and has an advantage over the older generation in terms of skills.

However, people easily overlook the fact that outside the core areas of information technology, it is still important to impart experience that goes beyond this. To combine the different skills of the generations, the generations involved need to work together.

I 5.3 Information technology - orientation on the labor market

Contexts and phenomena on the labor market

- Special job and qualification offers
On the one hand, there are special, unusual job vacancies. On the other hand, there are often unconventional combinations of training and experience. For both sides, it is important to locate the relevant databases and make a comparison with the other side.

- Highly qualified and urgently needed workers
If the labor market reveals the need for highly qualified workers and the scarcity of corresponding offers, there are of course opportunities to earn good incomes.

- Tenured job holders
Many job holders can show off respectable incomes. Some of them like to say that their situation is the result of their individual performance. However, some of these people owe their income more to the expansion and preservation of vested rights, which are established with the help of trade unions and politicians, among others.

If these people were not bound by laws and collective agreements to protect vested rights, but were in individual competition for income, as is the case with many other employees, then they would probably have much less chance of being well paid than is possible with the help of vested rights. It is obviously easy for these people to ignore such a realization in order to be able to present their income as their individual success.

-       Seemingly offered jobs
It is to be expected that employment agencies will advertise jobs even though they have no jobs to offer. By doing this, employment agencies sometimes only collect data from applicants in order to be able to offer them immediately to specific job seekers. A characteristic of such fictitious job advertisements is that they appear to be concrete and quite comprehensively formulated so that as many applicants as possible feel addressed and make their application documents available.

This is a special variant of competition. If an employment agency collects data in order to be able to respond quickly to the demand for labor, it can be more successful than competing agencies that do not do so. It therefore makes sense for all employment agencies to collect such data in order to prevent competitive disadvantages.

Asking for labor to improve data collection from employment agencies can give the appearance of quantitative real economy growth. Some politicians are happy to succumb to this illusion when they think they can report a success, e.g. of economic development.

-       Oversupply of labor
If there is an oversupply of labor, it might be assumed as a first approximation that in order to achieve a balanced labor market, wages would have to fall by roughly the same proportion as the supply of labor would be too high. However, the labor market functions less linearly and more erratically. If there is a noticeable

oversupply of workers, they must expect the supply of wages to fall disproportionately as long as other workers are willing to work for less and less money, perhaps out of necessity.

If there is an oversupply of workers, companies can often find some who are willing to work for very low pay. They are often given the hope of permanent employment and more money if they have proven themselves. However, this hope can be deceptive if other applicants are willing to work again for low pay and hope.

Jobseekers may have to repeatedly prove to people on temporary contracts that they deserve the chance to keep a paid job. Repeated failure is likely to shape many people's sense of worth.

People conditioned in this way may then develop adapted skills for organizing their lives. They may wean themselves off the world of work or they may not even have experienced the structure of life through paid work.

As a result, when evaluating the supply of employees on the labor market, it is often assumed that employees are not willing to work. These are often people who have repeatedly experienced over time that they are hardly needed.

If the labor market is left to its own devices for a long time, people often cannot be taken on in the world of work or they have to work for wages that are far too low. It is then necessary to enable the labor market to function properly due to possible resulting threats to social or state stability. This can be done by preventing societal polarization from getting out of hand. Growth gains would have to be distributed in such a way that not so much money is withdrawn from the real economy cycles that they weaken too much.

To reduce the weakness of the quantitative real economy it would make sense to replace proportional increases in income by an appropriately more equal distribution.

If a proportional increase in income increases polarization in the area of wealth and money thus ends up in speculative financial cycles, taxes on the resulting speculative profits can be used for redistribution in the direction of quantitative real economy growth.

Redistribution with the help of taxation would have to take place in very small steps so that redistribution can be stopped in time once societal polarization has been effectively limited.

I 5.4   Information technology - supply of goods

The supply of goods is still possible without the use of information technology. However, changes are becoming increasingly apparent. These are often partial, for example in that goods are ordered on the Internet, the provision of goods is largely controlled by information technology or payments are made via the Internet.

However, the ordering, provision and payment of goods are increasingly being carried out in a coherent manner with the help of information technology. As a result, complex organizational, technological and technical processes are becoming increasingly faster.

Significant amounts of time are then only required for the transportation and production of goods, devices, machines and automatic machines, insofar as these carry weight.

Control and regulation of goods, devices, machines and vending machines is largely carried out using information technology. Once the necessary programs have been created, they can be used again and again as copies for the same purpose without requiring a significant amount of time.

The work required to produce the hardware in particular is often carried out in low-income countries. Research, development, planning, organization and remaining work is often still carried out in industrialized countries with higher incomes The costs for production in and transport between the countries involved are optimized in terms of profitability. However, the environmental impact of additional transportation is rarely taken into account.

On the one hand, production in low-wage countries means that products manufactured there can be offered cheaply in industrialized countries. This makes it possible for parts of the population that have become relatively poor in industrialized countries within the framework of social polarization to be supplied cheaply.

On the other hand, production in the lowest-wage countries means that a large proportion of the population working there earns so little money that they can hardly afford quantitative goods. As a result, this part of the population is largely excluded from achieving growth and a certain level of comfort.

With increasing poverty, such a development can lead to instability and chaos in poor countries. This can result in a mass migration to the richer countries, which benefit from current account surpluses vis-à-vis the poor countries. The irony of this development is that high-tech products developed in industrialized countries can serve as a guide for people from poor countries in the direction of rich countries. The rich countries would probably like to prevent this, even if they earn money from the sale of these devices.

In the richer industrialized countries, there is a trend towards ever faster organizational processes made possible by information technology. This development is probably driven by the obvious desire to have needs met fabulously quickly. Just as fantastic depictions in science fiction novels became reality, today some wishes to obtain quantitative goods are fulfilled fabulously quickly.

In extreme cases, fairy-tale wishes and their realization coincide. Let us imagine the following case. The day before going to a party, we order a gift online that is to be delivered the next day. The next morning we find the order to provide the gift at our workplace in the company where we are employed and from which our private gift is to be provided. The extra work may mean that we are late for the party in the evening.

It is understandable that increasingly fast-paced organizational processes and the resulting concentration of work can become a burden for individuals and their lives together. One possible consequence of this is the burnout syndrome.

This development often appears in an inconspicuous guise. Thus, times, cost frameworks and workloads for jobs are often planned in such a way that the work to be done can hardly be completed without creating deadline pressure. With this type of work compression, it is often not possible to take a deep breath and relax. The resulting high blood pressure may even interfere with a good feeling of being active until the effects become apparent in the state of health or illness.

I 5.5   Information technology - Suppliers and consumers of goods

Sufficient quantitative real economy growth is characterized by the fact that quantitative goods tend to be scarce on the supply side, but their supply can follow demand. Scarcity must therefore enable the fulfillment of desires for such goods. A situation characterized by such scarcity should permit the parallel, adjusted increase in earnings and profits. This is an important condition for quantitative growth in the real economy.

Real economy growth can be stimulated, for example, by human curiosity, research and development. Innovative goods can be created in such an environment. On the one hand, this awakens the desire to acquire such goods. On the other hand, people should not be overburdened by the new and unknown. It would make sense to introduce and acquire innovative goods together along with their integration into tradition and experience. In times of quantitative real economy growth, advertising plays a special role in publicizing innovative goods and integrating them into the feeling of security conveyed by tradition. It wants to demonstrate the advantages of new innovative goods to buyers and possibly create a sense of challenge and adventure without creating uncertainty and being overburdened by the new.

If sufficient quantitative real economic growth turns into insufficient growth, real economic cycles can come to a standstill. Too many goods are then offered and too few goods are demanded. In such times, suppliers of goods are looking for buyers and other people are looking for sources of income when employment is weakening. This is where traditional demand-generating advertising enters the picture.

At the interface between suppliers and buyers, on the one hand people try to advertise their qualifications with the help of information and discover employment opportunities for themselves.

On the other hand, other people try to earn money in an information-oriented way. Information is obtained by identifying consumer habits in order to generate promising advertising measures for the sale of quantitative goods.

I 5.6 Information technology – Breaking down secrecy

Information is an essential part of private, social, technical, economic and political matters, for example. Using information technology, it is possible to collect, network, link, process and evaluate information to an increasing extent and increasingly quickly. Knowledge is gained that plays a role in a wide variety of contexts.

Special variants of information are those that express the value of money through a number and its currency. This information can be used to denote the value of quantitative goods. They also indicate the extent to which goods can be acquired. In the real economy, money as an information carrier is related to various phenomena.

If there is sufficient quantitative growth in the real economy, almost all people involved in the goods market are able to use money to fulfill their wishes for participation in growth gains to a sufficient amount.

If there is a lack of quantitative growth in the real economy, the desire for sufficient participation in growth gains obviously remains. If, in the case of automation, rationalization, partial unemployment, partially declining incomes and a tendency towards overproduction, quantitative real economy growth weakens and the growth gains to be distributed are no longer sufficient to satisfy all those involved, additional asymmetrical distribution of growth successes has a reinforcing effect. People who are then no longer able to participate in real economy cycles to a sufficient extent are the losers. Other people have enough potential in terms of education, qualifications, income and wealth to continue to participate increasingly in real economy cycles. Societal polarization is taking place between people.

This polarization can be intensified if people with higher incomes withdraw money from the real economy cycles by saving, and thus further weakening them.

These people will possibly use their money to achieve success in speculative financial cycles. Speculatively acquired money could be withdrawn from these people and quickly returned to the real economy cycles through redistribution. This would drive quantitative real economy growth and the widely based distribution of growth gains could be continued.

Obviously, this kind of redistribution is not practicable to the extent required because politicians are probably afraid of not being re-elected by people who would be deprived of speculatively acquired money by the state for redistribution to poorer people. This calls for further reflection on how to combat different types of polarization. To this end, information-centered measures are examined.

A central aspect of this consideration is that in times of sufficient quantitative growth in the real economy, individual interests in participating in growth successes for almost all members of society can flow together into a quasi-overall social interest and be satisfied. This supports social stability and acceptance of democracy.

In times of insufficient quantitative real economy growth, polarization of various kinds can arise. The satisfaction of individual interests in the sense of maintaining growth successes then no longer takes place to a sufficient extent for many members of society. This can lead to tensions between the emerging social groups - the disadvantaged and the advantaged.

At this point, the question arises as to how the beneficiaries on the one hand and the disadvantaged on the other behave in a polarizing society when interests are bundled into groups with the help of information technology.

On the one hand, there is the group of beneficiaries who want to continue to gain advantages in the face of weakening quantitative real economic growth. This happens, among other things, when politicians, in anticipatory obedience, carry out the corresponding social design, e.g. in the form of shaping and codifying the preservation of vested rights.
Apart from the beneficiaries of social polarization, there are also the disadvantaged. These could network in order to reduce social polarization in their favor using information technology

Just as advantage-takers in a polarizing society collect data on the consumption and lifestyle habits of citizens in order to use this knowledge to do better business, groups of disadvantaged people could collect democratically legitimized data on advantage-takers in order to influence their drive for social polarization. The drive lies in the secrecy within a competition-oriented real economy.

Secrecy not only accompanies the competitive society, but also the social polarization that develops from it. Supported by information technology, the drive for social polarization could be weakened by democratically legitimized relaxation of secrecy. Perhaps this would result in depolarization. At the same time, further considerations are logically important to ensure that depolarization does not lead to social instability.

I 5.6.1   Reducing secrecy in income structures

Income is often kept secret. This means that differences in income can remain hidden under the guise of secrecy. Companies can thus pay their employees different wages and salaries without creating tensions between them. Employees who earn more than others do not have to justify this. Employees who earn less than others therefore have nothing to be ashamed of.

Each individual employee is only confronted with his or her own expectation or those of their immediate environment. These expectations can mean that you want or should receive more money. Realized expectations are then a driving force for a growth-oriented competitive society.

In times of a weakening real economy, companies are tempted to pay the lowest possible wages and salaries, provided that some people are prepared to work for them. Growth gains are then primarily distributed to those who are needed because of their qualifications.

This creates a polarization between people whose incomes tend to fall and those whose incomes tend to rise.

As will be shown below, the fall in income levels that leads to poverty can be countered.

Minimum wages, for example, can be set for this purpose.
-	These can lead to higher prices and export reductions in exporting countries This would make it possible to limit current account surpluses on the one hand and current account shortfalls on the other, as well as the polarization between people in rich and poor countries.
-	Minimum wages can also reduce polarization within regions. They would have to be high enough to not only prevent poverty for the poor recipients, but also make the price increases resulting from minimum wages affordable for them. Furthermore, the price increases would also have to be borne by the richer citizens. For them, this would reduce the growth-inhibiting savings opportunities. The bottom line would be a reduction in societal polarization.

Minimum wages should only be increased slowly, in coordination with social and global polarization reduction, in order to avoid an overreaction in the real economy.

In addition to the described application of minimum wages for the purpose of reducing polarization, a company-oriented variant is also possible. To this end, companies could specify how many employees they pay a company minimum wage that exceeds the poverty-promoting level and at what level. The resulting price increases could also be specified in this context. This transparency would give the customers of these companies the chance to accept such corporate practices. Consumers could show to what extent they have compassion not only for nature and animals but also for people with too little income. Large companies in particular would have the potential to successfully launch and sustain such a campaign.

Wages and salaries also increase at initiative of trade unions. The increases are usually on a percentage basis. The incomes affected therefore diverge, as people with higher incomes receive more in percentage income increases than those with lower incomes. Polarization takes place. This process would be less severe if, in the event of income increases, the higher earners were given hardly any more additional money than the lower earners. E Equal distribution of income increases would then take precedence over proportional distribution.

The practice of predominantly proportional income increases is suggesting that the higher earners are more likely to hold the levers of the trade unions. By increasing incomes as a proportion, they are obviously also serving their own interests in achieving the highest possible increases in their incomes, instead of driving distribution towards poorer earners through more equal distribution. In this way, trade unions help to prevent possible additional consumption by poorer people, which could drive real economy cycles and thus help to increase growth gains that would again be available to all people.

It should be noted that proportional increases in wages and salaries lead to low-income earners remaining at a comparatively low-income level. It therefore seems logical that these people are always calling for income increases. In In their wake, high-earning trade union members are always able to earn disproportionately high wages, apparently inconspicuously.

It should be considered whether the disclosure of the income structure for the sector in question should be made mandatory before collective bargaining in order to ensure transparency for income negotiations and thus possibly provoke social pressure for more equal distribution.

I 5.6.2   Reducing secrecy in the purely speculative-financial sector

Assets can be divided into tangible assets and financial assets.

Tangible assets are, for example, land or buildings and factories. These assets are not discussed in any detail here.

In the following, financial assets are examined. They can arise from shares of income that are withheld from the consumption cycle and thus from the real economy through saving. This process can weaken quantitative real economy growth. However, saved money can still be fed into the real economy as follows and thus ensure quantitative real economic growth.

-    Firstly, some of the money saved can be redistributed directly into the real economy.
-    Secondly, financial assets that have been built up through saving can be taxed so that the taxes can then be fed into the real economy.
-    Thirdly, returns on speculative savings can be taxed and these taxes can be fed into the real economy.

The direct or indirect redistribution of saved money into the real economy, which appears to be quite sensible with regard to further quantitative growth of the real economy and the associated desired distribution of growth successes, can cause mistrust about the use of the money among those from whom the saved money is withdrawn. However, it is necessary to have confidence in the process of redistribution. This is the only way to lay the foundations for continuous quantitative growth in the real economy for generations to come. If sustainability cannot be guaranteed, some people will have to give up financial assets at time 1, which should generate further quantitative real economy growth. If the redistribution is not continued to the required extent at a later point in time 2 by those then active in the real economy, no corresponding growth gains can be made available to the old people of point in time 1. If reliability over generations cannot be considered to be guaranteed, the skepticism of those from whom money is to be withdrawn for redistribution purposes is understandable. As a result, they tend to prefer financial assets as a private building block for securing their future.

This means that social polarization between rich and poor people will continue. Richer members of society increasingly expand their individual financial assets and thus create a feeling of a secure future for themselves. If more and more people act like this, societal dissatisfaction arises among poor people and societal polarization increases. This also relates to secrecy, which is a central element of a competitive society from which its beneficiaries receive their polarizing income.

As long as real economic cycles increase, growth is sufficient, more and more money is earned and more and more goods are bought, the competitive society driven by secrecy unfolds its inherent strengths.

In times of insufficient quantitative real economy growth, societal polarization can emerge. It is partly driven by the combination of falling incomes on the one hand and savings, growing financial assets and speculative successes on the other. However, this development often takes place under the cloak of secrecy.

This gives rise to the idea that information technology could bring together the interests of people who are dissatisfied with the disadvantageous effects of societal polarization. As a result, the idea of democratically legitimizing the use of information technology to soften secrecy as a driver of polarization could develop, particularly in the purely speculative financial sector.

I 5.7 Information technology - Orientation aid for refugees

The trade between industrialized countries and newly industrialized countries often leads to poverty in these countries as a result of current account deficits, debt and interest payments. This can be the preliminary stage to dissatisfaction, instability, authoritarian forms of government and non-governability.

In response to these phenomena, democratic industrialized countries often demand democratic development and good governance from poor countries that are running out of control.

However, behind the curtain of such often rather superficial demands, richer industrialized countries primarily have a rational interest in supporting people and power structures in poor countries that serve the vested interests and advantages of the richer states. In this context, it is often ignored that the threat of social instability in poor countries can be the result of real economy developments that are favored by the measures taken by rich industrialized countries. Some aspects of this are outlined below:

-   When rich industrialized countries have current account surpluses, poorer countries on the other side of the trade chain can become over-indebted if they have to repay the loans taken out for imports plus the interest incurred without having set in motion self-sustaining real economic development in the poor countries. In this case, primarily the richer industrialized countries benefit from the current account surplus.

- Raw materials are often exported cheaply from poorer countries instead of being processed in the exporting countries to promote employment. If the processing takes place in the importing richer industrialized countries, then these benefit from the additional employment, from the purchasing power created and from the resulting quantitative real economic growth.

- Agricultural products from poorer countries often compete with subsidized products from richer industrialized countries. Instead of enabling poorer countries to have market-oriented export opportunities, these are obstructed by the non-market economy activities of richer countries. This is particularly true when agricultural subsidies in the richer countries are paid for from the successes of the current account surpluses that develop in relation to the poorer countries.

These real economic developments can lead to over-indebtedness, impoverishment of the population and authoritarian governments in poorer countries. In order to maintain state stability, such autocratic forms seem almost inevitable. They can also result in the ungovernability of states and warlike activities.

The populations of impoverished states are sometimes well informed about the standard of living in richer countries thanks to information technology. Particularly in this context, it is only logical that parts of the populations of impoverished countries are migrating towards the richer countries, which, as beneficiaries of current account surpluses, are expanding their wealth in relation to the poorer countries.

J   The economy in societal interaction

The economy is an important part of a society. It is considered here under the following terms:
- Protection of vested rights - Demography
- Real economy - purely speculative financial economy - economy of begging
- Birth rate - Resources
- Democracy - Freedom / Liberalism

J 1   Protection of vested rights - Demography

In times of sufficient real economy growth, growth gains increase by definition to a sufficient extent for almost all people involved. Purchasing power and profits are growing gradually. The people involved can be largely satisfied

- Societal polarization

Societal polarization can be caused by a number of partially interacting factors. These include automation, rationalization, the proportional distribution of growth gains and the protection of vested rights

Automation and rationalization can make some people unemployed - for them, income and purchasing power possibly decrease. On the other hand, other people's incomes increase if they are needed for automation and rationalization. At the same time, their purchasing power and savings opportunities will also increase.

This shows a divergence in income, purchasing power and wealth.

For instance, if the increase in income is expressed as a proportion, some population groups achieve greater gains than others.

We see a divergence in income, purchasing power and wealth.

For some population groups, collective wage agreements or statutory regulations ensure the protection of vested rights. This often includes rights and entitlements for the future. Trade unions and politicians are obviously tempted to use vested rights to attract certain parts of the population. The protection of vested interests influences the distribution of growth gains. If these decline when the quantitative real economy is weakening, but the status quo is fixed for a part of the population, this means that those who maintain the status quo are favored, while other population groups benefit relatively little from the remaining growth gains. These are the people with too little or no education, training or qualifications - but they are also the people with a lack of resilience or those with disabilities.

Again, there is a divergence in income, purchasing power and wealth.

Those parts of the population whose income and purchasing power tend to decline are provided with a minimum of financial support in order to limit their incentive for social dissatisfaction.

- New group configurations

As the demographic development progresses, the composition of the population changes. For biological reasons, the older population group is declining. Despite a low birth rate, the younger part of the population will therefore outnumber the older part of the population over time. The younger generation's participation in the real economy is partly restricted by the vested interests of some of the older generation. At the same time, the older generation likes to classify younger people as disenchanted with politics. The disenchantment with politics is perhaps just an expression of being tired of the older generation's efforts to polarize society.

What happens if the younger economically active generation forms a group together with the less fortunate in a weakening real economy? - A group of calculating righteous is formed. This group could gain a political majority in the course of demographic development and reform the protection of vested rights. This concerns the protection of vested rights, which derive their claims from times of sufficient quantitative real economic growth, but which realize their claims in times of insufficient quantitative economic growth at the cost of younger people and the disadvantaged.

J 2   Real economy - purely speculative financial economy - economy of begging

Initially, the following terms and, if necessary, their interrelationships are explained: Real economy, purely speculative financial economy, economy of begging, money, intellectual labor, physical labor, sufficient quantitative real economic growth, insufficient quantitative real economy growth.

- Real economy and the money
In the real economy, money is used, among other things, to buy or sell goods. It is a part of real economy cycles that are formed by the flow of goods in one direction and the flow of money in the opposite direction.

- Purely speculative financial economy
In the purely speculative financial sector, people sometimes try to make money with money. This can possibly be promoted by trading shares in companies with high frequency. The rapid buying and selling probably creates an illusion of scarcity with regard to these shares. As a result, buying impulses resulting from a scarcity-oriented market economy approach might be triggered for such shares. They often do not wait for profits in the form of distribution payments for the shares. Rather, potential price gains

are realized in advance, which may be provoked by rising demand for shares.

- Economy of begging and money

In the context of the economy of begging, money is only moved in one direction, namely from the giver to the taker, i.e. to the beggar, if the latter sends out signals of begging.

- Intellectual work

Intellectual work is the mental input required for considerations, research, inventions, development, organization, automation and rationalization.

- Physical labor

Physical·labor·is the work performed·within·one·time unit. It is provided as human physical labor and as machine physical labor.

- Merging intellectual work and physical labor

Intellectual work is the basis for a complex technological development. Initially, machines were invented and manufactured that could provide mechanical physical labor. More complex machines were developed into machinery. Furthermore, automation and rationalization are added by means of intellectual work. There is an increasing merging of intellectual work and mechanical physical labor. Humans are thus given an amplification factor, expressed by the ratio of mechanical physical to human physical labor.

The combination of intellectual work, human and mechanical physical labor, automation and rationalization increases the productivity in the manufacture of consumer and capital goods. For those involved, the supply of quantitative goods and the maintenance of growth successes can increase. People with high incomes can save money, which is available for investment in the growing real economy.

The combination of intellectual work, human and mechanical physical labor, automation and rationalization can lead to a tendency towards market saturation, unemployment and a partial reduction in income as a result of the ensuing increases in productivity. At the same time, there is an increase in income for people who are still needed for automation and rationalization to ensure competitiveness, for example. They can continue to save money.

-       Varying degrees of quantitative real economy growth and
        saved money
In times of sufficient quantitative growth in the real economy, money saved is used, among other things, for:
--   Investments in the production of quantitative goods
--   the purchase of expensive goods
These are real economic uses with longer usage or acquisition horizons. Both money saved and corporate profits can help to increasingly drive quantitative real economic growth. However, growth can also start to weaken at some point.
If saved money is no longer needed to a sufficient extent for investments in times of insufficient quantitative real economic growth, the expectation of receiving a return on saved money remains. In this context, the purely speculative use of saved money is a good option. This means that purely speculative money is used to obtain additional money by attempting to increase the amount of money invested through the process of moving money - buying and selling shares in companies, for example.

-       Different degrees of quantitative real economic growth and
        intellectual labor
Intellectual work is necessary in times of sufficient quantitative real economic growth in order to keep the real economy functioning.

Intellectual work is required in the event of insufficient quantitative real economic growth in order to maintain a competitive advantage in the real economy so as not to be forced out of the market by competing companies. Intellectual work is required in the event of insufficient quantitative real economic growth in order to maintain a competitive advantage in the real economy so as not to be forced out of the market by competing companies.

- Varying degrees of quantitative real economic growth and physical labor output

Physical labor is required in times of sufficient quantitative real economic growth in the real economy in order for it to be able to function.

Physical labor is also necessary in times of insufficient quantitative real economic growth in the real economy in order to maintain it.

- Lack of quantitative real economic growth and the purely speculative financial economy

If there is a lack of quantitative real economic growth, this is easily supplemented by a monetary spin-off, which can manifest itself as a purely speculative financial economy. In addition to purely speculative investments, this purely speculative financial economy requires intellectual work to design creative speculation strategies. This purely speculative financial economy hardly requires any weighty materials, whereas this is often the case in the real economy. This means that processes in the purely speculative financial sector are usually much faster than in the real economy and create speed-related problems.

- The pure speculative financial economy and the economy of begging

We next look at begging for money in relation to the speculative use of money. Where appropriate, both phenomena are considered in conjunction with intellectual labor, physical labor and varying degrees of quantitative real economy growth.

Where appropriate, both phenomena are considered in conjunction with intellectual labor, physical labor and varying degrees of quantitative real economy growth.

Physical labor is hardly required for begging or for the purely speculative use of money.

In times of sufficient quantitative growth in the real economy, begging is probably less popular, because the possibility of a better and more comfortable life with more and more work in the real economy and more and more money earned means that begging tends to fade into the background.

In times of insufficient qualitative real economy growth, begging can become an existential necessity.

Begging and the speculative use of money are attempts to achieve benefits.

In the begging economy, the beggar's benefit is realized by redistribution upon the donor's consent.

In the purely speculative financial sector, those involved are obviously hoping that in the game to achieve capital gains, the losers may not be them but others.

J 3   Birth rate - Resources

In wealthy industrialized countries, there are popular thinking patterns about central problems in poor countries. These relate, for example, to child wealth and poverty.

According to these thinking patterns, the parents' desire to have a number of children stems from their need to prevent foreseeable poverty. A larger number of children should serve to secure the future and thereby also limit poverty.

Following on from this idea, it can be concluded that the distribution of money earned and goods produced among many people - including children - can lead to poverty.

Here we are facing a special variant of the cause-and-effect correlation. Firstly, in the context of poverty, the thoughts and actions of many people create a great number of children. Secondly, the distribution of money and goods results in poverty as a social phenomenon and obviously favors the growing number of children.

Poverty and the abundance of children are mutually reinforcing, as in a circle. Let us try a thought experiment. In the past, in order to reduce poverty, the rich countries would have had to pay the poorer countries appropriately higher wages for production work and appropriately higher prices for raw materials and goods over a long period of time. This would have significantly reduced poverty. Of course, it should be borne in mind that education and infrastructure, for example, would also have had to develop. However, this kind of real economy development would have led to an increase in the consumption of environmental resources in particular in poorer countries.

Now the question may be asked whether the previously accepted poverty as a consequence of the prevention of real economy growth in poor countries was carried out by the rich countries as a simple realization of real economy advantages, or whether long-term planning of the stretching of resource stocks was already a consideration in the background. The existence of poverty and child poverty in some countries has to be stated.

In the current situation, a transition period is required from poverty with an abundance of children to increasing prosperity with a lower proportion of children in the population. The population is expected to stagnate or decline over time. Then the money generated could be divided among fewer people.

Given the limited resources available, it is important to think further ahead:

Resource consumption on earth is currently unevenly distributed. A smaller proportion of the world's population realizes a larger share of total resource consumption. However, a larger proportion of the world's population can currently only claim a smaller share of resource consumption. This means that, mainly in the richer industrialized countries, several times more resources are consumed per person compared to people in poorer countries.

With regard to resource consumption by poor and rich countries, there are at least two possibilities for adjustment

- People in poorer countries could claim their right to achieve the same standard of possession and acquisition of quantitative goods as richer people in richer countries. This would mean that the poorer countries would require a higher consumption of resources in the future. For the entire human population, the question then arises as to how long the resource of the environment available for consumption could keep up with the resulting growth.

- In an alternative thought process, the question can be asked as to how many people could live in Germany, for example, if the average person there did not use more resources than the average person in poorer countries. In this case, a greater number of people could live in Germany without using more resources than with a lower population and higher resource consumption per person.

In order to preserve the supply of resources for the future, there are two necessities. Firstly, the rich industrialized countries must reduce their consumption of resources. Secondly, the birth rate must fall in poor, barely industrialized countries. To this end, it would be logical to at least pay for the products in poorer countries in such a way that old-age provision could be built up there as a substitute for an abundance of children.

J 4   Democracy – Freedom / Liberalism

Democracy can serve as a set of rules for a society and thus also for the associated real economy. Democracy should ensure that the desire for freedom of individuals can be limited to such an extent that almost all people can live together as peacefully and equally as possible.

Under the cover of freedom and liberalism, freedom of speech and freedom of money can be found, and freedom-loving people are happy to make use of them.

The "freedom of the word" can make it possible to coordinate society.

The freedom of money can lead to the development of societal polarization and democracy as a set of rules reaching its limits. Such is the case, for example, if it is not possible to tame societal polarization, which can manifest itself as an outgrowth of the real economy and especially the purely speculative financial economy.

The following shows that in a competition-based real economy, democracy often only has the option to react to undesirable developments in the real economy.

J 4.1   Democracy and freedom / liberalism belong together - but are drifting apart

First thesis: By describing qualitative goods, quantitative goods, money and the exchange processes that take place, human co-existence and human activity can be described.

Second thesis: Democracy allows freedom of thought and action. The liberal behavior of some people must not restrict the liberal behavior of others by too much. In this field of mutual relations between the people involved, democracy offers the practice of freedom.

Freedom of action encompasses the exchange of qualitative goods and the production, sale and purchase of quantitative goods, restricted by the rules of democracy.

The previous statements describe the actions of people with a liberal orientation who form the democratic state. Thus, when we talk about freedom and liberalism, we are talking about qualitative goods, quantitative goods, money and their exchange.

This correlation can also be visualized as follows. Free action, thinking, research and organization and, as a result, technical progress and the improved comfort of life take place with the help of qualitative and quantitative goods that are produced, exchanged and traded in a democratic environment.

In times of sufficient quantitative real economy growth, the advantages of participating in growth gains in the form of quantitative goods and money are gladly realized in alongside qualitative goods.

In times of insufficient quantitative growth, the handling of quantitative goods seems to be changing, as will be shown below.

The freedom to produce quantitative goods using automation and rationalization can increasingly lead to societal and global polarization, especially if growth gains are distributed asymmetrically. They show up between:

-    people with paid work and people without paid work
-    people with sufficient income and people with insufficient income
-    people with assets to bridge financially difficult times and people without assets

- people with sufficient security for the future and people without sufficient security for the future
- countries with current account surpluses and those with current account deficits
- countries with many relatively rich people and countries with very many relatively poor people
- Countries with a stable democracy in the context of a real economy that provides well for the population and poor countries with a poor real economy that may give rise to hotbeds of unrest or authoritarian rule.

The negative consequences of societal polarization are understandably rejected primarily, but are obviously not sufficiently combated by the beneficiaries through accumulated individual countermeasures.

J 4.2   Democracy, freedom / liberalism and variants of polarization

The beneficiaries of societal polarization may try to justify their advantages by claiming that they arise within the framework of liberal democracy. The people who are disadvantaged by societal polarization should obviously accept the negative consequences within the framework of liberal democracy. This is where the liberal behavior of some unduly restricts the behavior of others. Possible social tensions have the potential to jeopardize liberal democracy. That is why it is important to analyze the situation.

- Moralistic reaction

As a reaction to societal polarization, rich people are often blamed by poorer people for the rise of polarization and especially for its consequences. In the name of justice, it seems appropriate to make morally justified demands stating that poorer people should be able to participate sufficiently in real economic growth gains at the expense of richer people.

\-   Stability-oriented reaction

There is also the stability-oriented demand for redistribution, especially of money saved by people with higher incomes. The money should be channeled into the hands of poorer people so that it can be quickly transferred from there into real economic consumption in order to enable new quantitative real economy growth and new growth gains for everyone involved. In this way, the satisfaction of all people involved and the stability of the liberal democratic state supported by them is to be maintained.

If morally oriented or stability-oriented demands for redistribution were realized on a large scale, a new polarization would be created. This is an ecological polarization driven by real economy growth and resource consumption that occurs between the two times discussed below.

\-   The time of sufficient resources

On the one hand, it is possible to imagine a time when there is enough energy, raw materials and the environment required for consumption to enable permanent quantitative real economy growth. Sufficient qualitative and quantitative goods and growth gains could then be available for all those involved so that these people are prepared to support the liberal democratic state if it fulfills the accompanying community tasks and ensures stability.

\-   The time of insufficient resources

On the other hand, there is the time when resources to be distributed sometimes become too scarce. These can be resources of energy and raw materials and in particular the resource of the environment that can be used for consumption.

Limited resources can lead to fights over distribution. These may initially be partly regulated by the market. However, distribution fights can also have different results, as outlined below:

- Migration as applied democracy

The participation of poor people or poor parts of the population in the growth gains of rich people or rich nations could be made possible through an information technology-supported migration of peoples. This is a form of applied democracy in which people vote with their feet.

This would fulfill the requirement of economically successful democratic states to practice democracy. This demand is not linked to a call for mass migration, but rather implies the demand to largely accept the status of poverty and to practice democracy in one's own country with this in mind.

- Fights over the distribution of resources can have early causes that only later have existential, unstoppable consequences

The scarcity of the resource of the environment available for consumption is characterized in particular by the time at which its consumption can have existential consequences for parts of the earth or the whole earth that can hardly be stopped. Of course, we may speculate as to whether such a development takes place in stages or is locally limited, whether counter-movements become effective in time or whether the consumption of the overall available environment progresses unstoppably from a certain time onwards.

People might ask themselves whether they want to put on the shoe of cynical behavior by apparently relying on the fate-driven, time-optimized mercy of a timely death in order to avoid being held accountable later in an international court for causing hunger and environmental destruction.

However, all people could also think about how hunger and poverty and the consumption of resources that jeopardize livelihoods - especially environmental resources - could be reduced to secure livelihoods.

K   Interim result

To summaries, everything that people exchange, give or acquire can be divided into qualitative or quantitative goods. The goods without a monetary value are qualitative goods. Qualitative goods are simply exchanged. The goods with a monetary value are quantitative goods. They can be sold or purchased with money.

Developments in the real economy can be illustrated on the basis of the acquisition of quantitative goods and the quantitative real economy growth realized therewith.

On the one hand there are the times of sufficient quantitative real economy growth People involved can then maintain sufficiently high growth gains and thus not only ensure their survival, but also increasingly treat themselves to comfort. They might even be able to acquire status symbols. This creates the conditions for a contented, stable and democratic society. However, such a development seems to have natural limits.

Constantly increasing quantitative real economy growth results in a constantly increasing consumption of resources. This applies in particular to the resource "environment". This creates an ecological polarization driven by resource consumption. It takes place between two times. The first time is the starting point. It is characterised by the fact that resources then start to diminish faster than the earth can replenish them. The second time is the point at which the consumption of environmental resources in particular begins to have irreversible global consequences that jeopardize the existence of the company. In order to effectively mitigate such a development, it seems logical to slow down quantitative real economy growth in time and sufficiently.

Besides the above idea of sufficient quantitative real economy growth, the phenomenon of insufficient quantitative real economy growth must also be considered. Insufficient growth can be caused by the fact that people receive little money or that they become unemployed due to rationalization and automation and their earnings tend to decrease. Then their available purchasing power weakens. If, at the same time, wages, salaries and incomes continue to rise for other people and they save part of it, they are withdrawing money from the consumption cycle. Both the weakening purchasing power of one group and the savings of the other weaken the consumption cycle.

If phenomena of drifting incomes become more pronounced, this can lead to societal polarization:
- between people with sufficiently paid work and those who have no or too little paid work,
- between people with sufficient or too little income,
- between people without assets and those with assets,
- between people, whose differences are amplified by percentage increases in wages, salaries and incomes,
- between countries with a current account surplus and those with a current account deficit.

Taking a group-oriented view, we see that groups of people emerge as those who ...
- have too little to eat, so they go hungry,
- only feed themselves from their own farming,
- can only receive very inadequate medical care,
- cannot build up reserves for bottlenecks when wages are low,
- rely on goods from countries with the lowest wages for their own low wages,
- are dependent on help with low wages,
- receive sufficient income,
- receive high incomes or own assets.

The people mentioned live in a wide variety of countries, which can be characterized as follows. There are countries ...
- with predominantly very poor people,
- with a mix of poor people and people with sufficient resources,

- with a mix of adequately and well to very well provided for people.

So there are different degrees of polarization that can be seen between people within countries and between countries. The question arises as to how the process of polarization can be made transparent, how it might develop further and how to intervene if necessary.

In times of sufficient quantitative real economy growth, politicians can redistribute growth gains to fulfil community tasks and in favor of disadvantaged social groups, thus helping to underpin social satisfaction.

In times of insufficient quantitative real economy growth, in which the first limits to the ability to influence growth are becoming apparent, politicians clearly lack the courage to continue effective financial redistribution in favor of the weakest consumers. Redistribution should probably serve to keep the growing real economy moving in such a way that all people can participate in growth gains, have enough to eat and can live decently. Politicians do not seem to have the confidence to pursue a path of further growth-effective redistribution because they are afraid of being considered unelectable by the beneficiaries of polarization if they have to accept losses for the sake of redistribution.

If some politicians seem to have run out of time for waffling on redistribution, there is a temptation for them to mutate into so-called populists. They can become crystallization points for a development that suggests it wants to tackle the causes of societal polarization.

The question arises as to what extent so-called populists really want to find out what drives social polarization. It is assumed that they focus on the disadvantaged, underachievers, foreigners or people from foreign cultures, for example, blaming them for social polarization and dissatisfaction and having their actions confirmed as correct by parts of the population from the populists' country.

If we take this idea to its logical conclusion, populists tend to take an authoritarian approach to undesirable developments in the real economy because they are unlikely to have any effective real economy solutions to the various forms of polarization that they can or want to implement.

At this point at the latest, it is necessary to look for ways in which the different variants of polarization can be influenced. This is done using the keywords depolarization and sustainability.

L   Opportunities for action - a summary

First, the variants of polarization that form the core of this book are briefly described.

-        The emergence of a first stage of polarization caused by diverging incomes that come along with real economic growth.

Different incomes can stimulate real economy growth. This can happen because higher income for one group can be an incentive for another to also receive more. Low incomes usually increase at the same time as higher incomes, with the gaps between the groups tending to widen. If such increases in income fit into the real economy cycles, different incomes act as a driver of real economy growth from which everyone involved can benefit.

The diverging income levels can form a first stage of societal polarization.

-        Societal polarization

Societal polarization can be intensified if consumer goods and capital goods can be produced increasingly quickly through automation and rationalization combined with the use of resources.

On the one hand, this requires a decreasing number of low-skilled people. They tend to receive less additional money.

On the other hand, people with the necessary qualifications are increasingly needed. These people receive increasingly more money and can save some of it.

This, together with the development described above, results in a divergence in income. This is a process of societal polarization between people with different incomes.

The process of societal polarization described in the context of technology and economy is further intensified by the asymmetrical and thus also proportional distribution of wage and salary increases, for example.

If too little money is fed into the consumptive cycles because wages and salaries are far too low for many people and because many other higher-income people save too much money, this will have an impact. If the real economy then weakens, the beneficiaries' demand for additional income can only be met primarily by imposing restrictions on disadvantaged people. In this context, a real economy involves a relative redistribution from the disadvantaged to the advantaged. This·also·reinforces·societal·polarization.

-        Ecological polarization
Ecological polarization can arise when people acquire an amplification factor with the help of automation and rationalization and thus continuously produce more consumer and capital goods. Resources such as raw materials, energy and the environment are increasingly being used. The use of raw materials and energy causes significant damage to the environment. In the course of time, the consumption of resources leads to ecological polarization. It mainly concerns the resource "environment" and develops between two points in time, i.e. it has a temporal dimension. The first point in time is characterized by the fact that the amount of resources used becomes greater than the amount that can be replenished by the earth. The second point of ecological polarization will be reached when resource consumption becomes a threat to our existence, perhaps even developing its own momentum and then no longer even requiring an external driver.

-        Global polarization
Global polarization is mainly reflected in the emergence of poor and rich countries and in the very different quantities of goods and resources available to the polarized countries.

Rich countries can influence global polarization. On the one hand, they can do this by paying low prices to poor countries for the supply of raw materials and agricultural products and for the manufacture of their products. On the other hand, poor countries have to pay high prices to rich industrialized countries.

As a result, poor countries receive little money to purchase goods and indirectly for the related consumption of resources. If rich countries thus succeed in minimizing the consumption of resources by poor countries, the rich countries can extend their time horizon for the supply of resources.

In the context of societal, ecological and global polarization, instruments for depolarization and sustainability are now being identified in order to limit them.

L 1   Depolarization tools

 The following tools for reducing polarization and achieving depolarization are presented:
- Minimum wages
- Preventive redistribution through more equally distributed wages and salaries
- Redistribution of speculative profits
- Redistribution between states - allow state bankruptcy

- Minimum wages
Minimum wages could be gradually increased until their recipients can live adequately on them. It would also make sense for minimum wages to be used to build up a pension scheme for their recipients, so that these people are not threatened with poverty in old age.

The prices for the products manufactured with the help of people earning minimum wages would have to be increased to such an extent that the increase in minimum wages can be guaranteed. The gradual increase in minimum wages should be slow enough to allow the goods market to adjust continuously.

The price increases would also have to be paid by the beneficiaries of societal polarization. This would put additional strain on the purchasing power of the beneficiaries. This results in an indirect redistribution from the beneficiaries towards people with too low an income. As a result, there is a partial reduction in societal polarization.

- Preventive redistribution through more equally distributed wages and salaries

One driver of societal polarization with its known negative consequences is the proportional increase in income. People with high salaries and wages receive a higher amount as a supplement than people with low salaries and wages. As a result, the income gap is widening. Societal polarization is being driven forward.

As an antidote to this development, it is advisable to replace proportional increases in wages and salaries in part with salary increases of the same amount. The increase in income for people with high wages and salaries would be weakened. There is a preventive redistribution from people with high wages and salaries towards people with wages and salaries that are too low. Societal polarization and its consequences would be mitigated.

In this regard, it would make sense to limit the instruments "minimum wages" and "more evenly distributed wages and salaries" in a stability-oriented manner, for example by taking the total wages and salaries of the previous year as a benchmark.

- Redistribution of speculative profits

It would seem sensible to redirect speculative successes towards the real economy to the extent that real economy growth is promoted to a sufficient extent. The redistribution should be carried out in such a way that the intended success of appropriate depolarization is observable and can be regulated.

- Redistribution between states - allow state bankruptcy
Between countries there is the interaction of current account surplus and current account deficit. If the gap between the two widens too much, this is a polarization phenomenon. Once a certain degree of polarization has been reached, it seems sensible to counteract this polarization by striking a balance between the states. A market-based solution would be to allow the insolvency of over-indebted, almost insolvent states. Lenders would thus have a central interest in avoiding the over-indebtedness of states in order to prevent the loss of loans granted following a state bankruptcy.

L 2   Sustainability tools

In a first step, we considered possibilities for reducing polarization and for achieving depolarization. They are designed to ensure that, with sufficient real economy growth, enough growth gains can be distributed to all stakeholders to guarantee social satisfaction and democratic stability.

The second step is to realize sustainability. This is required if quantitative real economy growth demands increasing resource consumption as a means of depolarization. As this ultimately leads to excessive consumption of environmental, raw material and energy resources, it is important to prevent such a development, especially for the key resource "environment". Sustainability can serve to effectively stretch the consumption of resources.

In this context, it is particularly important that a relatively long time can pass between the realization of environmental consumption and the existential consequences for people. The generations that caused it may already have died by the time the following generations are confronted with the consequences.

A sustainable real economy is required to decisively limit the consumption of resources. It includes the following measures: Use of renewable energy, recycling of raw materials and reduction of environmental consumption.

A sustainable real economy is based first and foremost on the use of renewable energy, which should be generated primarily where this is possible at optimum cost.

Recycling comes into play for the further development of a sustainable real economy. A special country type is recommended for this. In such countries, wages would sensibly be much lower than in traditional high-wage industrialized countries. On the one hand, the lower wages would have to be high enough for real economy cycles to exist to a sufficient extent. On the other hand, recycling would be more worthwhile with lower wages than in labor-intensive traditional industrialized countries.

Combining renewable energy and raw materials obtained through recycling would not only reduce the consumption of non-renewable energy with its implicit environmental damage, but also the consumption of raw materials from the resource reserve.

Investments in a sustainable real economy could be made by population groups that do not participate in the risks of speculative money cycles. The efficiency of such an alternative can be imagined if the lost values of burst financial bubbles had been invested sustainably.

Financial companies, which have to pay for the consequential damage caused by environmental destruction, are also naturally interested in sustainable investments. Large companies with corresponding potential could lead the way for sustainable real economic projects.

L 3   What's next?

As people want to survive, live better or live in luxury, there is a growing demand for goods: consumer goods and capital goods. If the growth required for this takes place in conjunction with money, it is called "quantitative real economy growth" in this book. The goods in question are then called "quantitative goods".

Growth gains achieved are usually distributed as a proportion in the form of increases in wages, salaries, interest and returns. The increases vary depending on the level of income and assets accumulated. As a result, some people have little or too little money at their disposal to live adequately. Other people can build up or inherit so much wealth that it is not needed overall for investment in real economy growth and can instead cause instability in speculative, purely financial economy cycles.

The divergence of income and wealth between people can lead to polarization within and between countries. Increasing polarization bears the risk of distribution struggles, distribution wars and refugee movements.

In order to curb the consequences of polarization in poor countries, authoritarian governments there can be supported by arms exports so that these governments can prevent polarization-related unrest.

Walls and fences can also be built against refugees or geological barriers such as seas can be used as natural borders against refugees.

As an alternative to the polarizing asymmetrical distribution of growth gains, this could be partially replaced by equal distribution. This could lead to increasing satisfaction among disadvantaged people and lay the foundations for a stable democratic state.

The equal distribution of growth gains, which promotes greater social stability and democracy, enables significantly more consumption and use of resources such as raw materials, energy and the environment worldwide. This consumption ultimately means a global threat to our existence. In order to counteract this development, we need to recycle, use renewable energy and, in particular, reduce our consumption of the environment.

If global quantitative real economy growth has to be limited due to the finite nature of the environment as a resource, there is obviously no market economy momentum that simply needs to be triggered.

The potential existential global threat posed by the consumption of environmental resources can develop its own momentum, especially because climate and water can move without limits. Climate change and marine pollution can therefore not be kept within limits.

For this reason, the competition for the described share of environmental consumption is analyzed. Consumption is realized by polluting the air and oceans, among other things. In this context, environmental protection serves to sufficiently reduce pollution of the air and oceans. As pollution of the air and oceans knows hardly any boundaries, all polluters would have to reduce pollution appropriately within their own borders. Countries A, which have so far produced little pollution per person with low prosperity, could insist that other countries B, which have so far produced a lot of pollution per person, have to make advance payments to reduce pollution. If country A wants to continue polluting in order to achieve an appropriate minimum level of prosperity and pollution hardly recognizes national borders, a conflict with country B would be obvious. This raises the important question of future interest-led cooperation between many countries.

Finally, the following far-reaching questions arise:

What does the global situation look like when the consumption of goods, raw materials, energy and the environment lead to a global existential threat?

Is there sufficient redistribution between people, groups and peoples polarized within the real economy?
Is there enough recycling of raw materials?
Is enough renewable energy available?
Can recycling and the use of renewable energy significantly limit environmental consumption?
If the required development is achieved by:
- democratically implemented regulations with a lighthouse function for many poorer countries?
- authoritarian military-based governments?
- information technology-based regimes?
- constraints that become effective in good time, triggered by excessive consumption of the environment
- activities of many idealists to reduce societal, global and ecological polarization, even if the beneficiaries of societal, ecological and global polarization continue as before?

Description of key terms used in the book

Qualitative goods

They can be exchanged without using money. These include human attention, recognition, communication and unpaid help. However, many products also have a qualitative character when they are exchanged without the use of money. For many qualitative goods, the exchange is negotiated. Mostly, they are simply given and taken.

Quantitative goods

These have a price assigned to them and can be sold and purchased for this price.

Financial resources / money

They are used to buy and sell quantitative goods. They can also be temporarily stored, lent to other people and borrowed from other people - often in form of interest payments.

Exchange economy

This is where qualitative goods are exchanged for other qualitative goods.

Consumer economy

It consists of quantitative goods intended for final consumption that can be purchased for money.

Real economy

It consists of quantitative goods. To buy and sell these goods, financial resources are required. Mostly, money is used as a means of payment. The real economy is a combination of quantitative goods and financial resources in real economy cycles. However, financial resources also become independent in the real economy-oriented financial sector, which is described below.

Real economy orientated financial management

In the financial economy, which is geared towards the real economy, financial resources are used to sell and purchase quantitative goods. Furthermore, the financial sector, which is geared towards the real economy, is used to carry out the intermediate storage of money, lending and borrowing required for the real economy to function.

Speculative financial management

It offers the incentive to potentially earn additional money through speculation. Initially, company shares may be purchased. These shares may only be intended to generate returns that are rendered by the companies. If the price of shares rises due to a good return, price gains may provide an incentive to sell shares and realize the price gains as well as the return. In this context, it can also be attractive to realize the resulting price gains in an atmosphere of rising prices without waiting for the yield payment. This development could possibly turn into purely speculative trading within the speculative financial sector. In order to separate speculative from purely speculative finance, a trading frequency can be defined for the transition

Information economy

Information can be collected, exchanged and exploited. They experience their central applicability in connection with information technology. The latter, in turn, is part of the information economy. There, information technology interacts with entertainment, games, the real economy and the speculative economy, for example. The secrecy of information supported by information technology and the resulting advantages are a driving force in the competitive real economy.

Human reinforcing factors

If people only have their physical energy at their disposal, they are busy ensuring their own survival to a very limited extent. If they produce goods using education, research, development, machinery, information technology as well as raw materials and external energy, a better survival becomes possible. The ratio of external energy to internal energy is the human reinforcing factor. It increases the consumption of external energy, raw materials and the environment.

Real economy drivers

The drivers are among others: Quantitative goods, human labor, current account surplus, waste of goods, consumption of resources, innovative products, status goods, recycling, environmental protection, investments, education, savings, loans and public community tasks. They interact with machinery and information technology. The important thing is human direction.

Growth gains

They are the amounts of money that are available due to the increase in quantitative real economy growth.

Sufficient quantitative real economy growth

The level of being sufficiently provided for by the real economy can be considered to have been reached when almost all of the people involved receive so much growth that they can recognize satisfaction. The level of sufficient
supply from the real economy can be considered to have been reached when almost all stakeholders achieve sufficient growth to show satisfaction. Furthermore, it is probably advisable to keep the hope of obtaining sufficient growth yields alive.

Stability and democracy

To guarantee social stability, it must be assumed that almost all members of society should participate sufficiently in qualitative and quantitative growth. Furthermore, the community tasks should be fulfilled on a democratic basis in order to secure the existence of democracy.

Insufficient quantitative real economy growth

This is reflected in the fact that too many members of a society receive too few growth gains and there is a risk of social dissatisfaction.

The global staircase

This can be imagined as a staircase where all the people on earth are trying to get to the top for a better life. So, on the way to the top, there is competition with other people. The issue is survival, abundance or hunger and wealth or poverty. People have different reinforcing factors in the form of money, energy and machines. They can thus provide themselves differently with consumer and capital goods. In this process takes places an increasing polarization between people - some people reach different levels at the top and others remain at different levels at the bottom.

Societal polarization

In the course of the real economy's development, societal polarization is gradually intensifying, driven by automation, rationalization and the increasingly asymmetrical distribution of growth gains. Societal polarization is evident between people with sufficiently paid work and those who have no or too little paid work; between people with sufficient and too little income; between people without assets and those with assets and between people who can only participate in the real economy to a very different extent due to asymmetrical increases in wages, salaries and income over time.

Global polarization

Global polarization is evident between countries with a current account surplus and those with an excessive current account deficit.

Ecological polarization

Ecological polarization can be described as developing between two points of time. The first time is characterized by the fact that resource reserves begin to diminish faster than they can regenerate or renew themselves. For the second point in time, the resource "environment" in particular has been used up to such an extent that the survival of many people is existentially jeopardized.

Depolarization

Depolarization is discussed here as a tool to combat different variants of polarization. These considerations are obvious because polarization can cause social and global tensions. An approach to influencing the various types of polarization is provided by information technology. This is due to the fact that the various types of polarization are driven, among other things, by competition in the real economy and the secrecy practiced in this process Confidential information unfolds its effectiveness when combined with information technology. It does not only offer the advantages of networkability, but is also characterized by vulnerability. Vulnerability could lead to a democratically legitimized reduction in secrecy, competitive advantages and various variants of polarization. This process is referred to as a democratically legitimizable depolarization tool.

Sustainability

Sustainability is defined here as ensuring the availability of resources in the form of energy, raw materials and the consumable environment over a long period of time. To this end, it makes sense to focus on locating industries where renewable energy is available at favorable conditions and where rather medium wage levels not only enable the real economy but also make recycling attractive. On the one hand, such locations with medium wage levels can serve as a model for low-wage countries that have so far subsidized high-wage countries with their low wages. On the other hand, countries with medium wage levels are likely to be a challenge for high-wage countries. Firstly, it appears obvious that they will continue to use polarization to keep a large proportion of people as poor as possible within the framework of polarization and thus keep them away from resource degradation. The rich countries could thus try to secure the resource reserves for themselves for as long as possible. However, foreclosing the consequences of climate change and marine pollution in favor of the rich countries hardly works.

Figure: Real economy drivers in a network

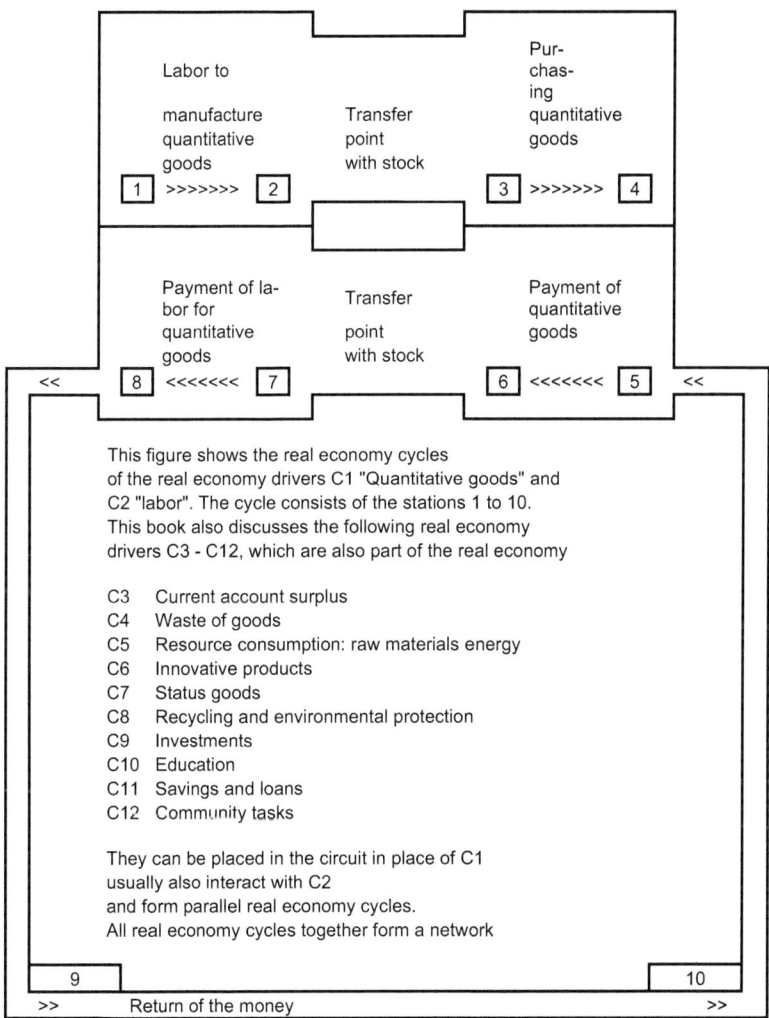

Labor to manufacture quantitative goods

Transfer point with stock

Purchasing quantitative goods

1 >>>>>>> 2

3 >>>>>>> 4

Payment of labor for quantitative goods

Transfer point with stock

Payment of quantitative goods

8 <<<<<<< 7

6 <<<<<<< 5

This figure shows the real economy cycles
of the real economy drivers C1 "Quantitative goods" and
C2 "labor". The cycle consists of the stations 1 to 10.
This book also discusses the following real economy
drivers C3 - C12, which are also part of the real economy

C3   Current account surplus
C4   Waste of goods
C5   Resource consumption: raw materials energy
C6   Innovative products
C7   Status goods
C8   Recycling and environmental protection
C9   Investments
C10   Education
C11   Savings and loans
C12   Community tasks

They can be placed in the circuit in place of C1
usually also interact with C2
and form parallel real economy cycles.
All real economy cycles together form a network

9   Return of the money   10

Publications of the author:
(All following publications are in German language)

Germany - Rwanda
Economic growth and consequences - approaches to resource-centered economics
publisher: *controller magazin*, 6/2012, p. 70 - 73

Time shown on the example of Central Europe and Rwanda
Understanding - self-sufficiency - learning - work - personal responsibility - uncertainty
publisher: *Zeitpresse* 3/2012, p. 35 – 37

Economization of relationships
Informational transparency - separation of bank liability - financial reorganization - depolarization
publisher: *Zeitpresse* 1/2012, p. 18 - 29

Polarizing changes
Systemic market failure on goods and financial markets in the event of inadequate economic growth - polarization - culture of envy - stability - democracy
publisher: *Zeitpresse* 1/2011, p. 32 - 38

Sufficiently strong economic growth - democratic stability - rationalization - lack of economic growth - changed financial markets-societal polarization - burden on the state - what's next?
publisher: *Zeitpresse*, summer 2009, p. 22 - 29

Asymmetric economic phenomena
publisher: *controller magazin*, 2007 special edition, p. 35 - 38

Asymmetric time
publisher: *Zeitpresse*, winter 2006/2007, p. 11 - 14

Controllers and insolvency prevention
Key controlling - observing signs jeopardizing company's existence
publisher: *controller magazin*, 2/2006, p. 181 -184

2024-05-26

Working in Afghanistan - the economic and cultural-socio-
logical context of poppy cultivation
Contribution to the 28. Federal Drug Congress 2005 in
Augsburg: www.fdr-online.info
Afghanistan - a field report
publisher: *controller magazin*, 1/2005, p. 93 - 94

Time and individuality in Germany and Afghanistan
publisher: *Zeitpresse*, winter 2004/2005, S. 20 - 25

New Economy and IT
Speed of complex economic and technical processes
publisher: *controller magazin*, 5/2002, p. 501 - 507

Time stress - time wasting - controlling
Managers in the balancing act between time-scarce economics and
time requirements to manage innovative complex development
publisher: *controller magazin*, 3/2001, p. 229 - 235

Companies in the expansion phase
Credit security and instruments for screening companies
publisher: *controller magazin*, 6/1998, p. 444 - 450

The system change in East Germany
Economic-psychological aspects of the system change
publisher: *Der Betriebswirt,* 3/1997, p. 23 - 26

Controlling in companies
Tools for recognizing the economic situation
publisher: *Mitteldeutsche Wirtschaft* 02/1997, p. 48 - 50

Concept against the impending wave of bankruptcies:
The hard way of doing
publisher: *Mitteldeutsche Wirtschaft* 12/1996, p. 12 - 14

Quality defects: Prevention is good, control is necessary
publisher: *Der Konstrukteur* 1-2/1988, p. 6 - 12

People-machine systems - automation changes planning processes
publisher: *Der Konstrukteur* 5/1987, p. 6 - 14

Good advice is expensive - bad advice can be expensive
1. Dubious management consultants and how to recognize them
   publisher: *Der Betriebsleiter* 10/1986, p. 6 - 10
2. Requirements for reputable consulting companies
   publisher: *Der Betriebsleiter* 11/1986, p. 6 - 9
3. Requirements for those seeking advice
   publisher: *Der Betriebsleiter* 12/1986, p. 6 - 8

Internal co-operation
Trust is good - mistrust is necessary
publisher: *BetriebsWirtschaftsMagazin* 2/1986, p. 39 – 43
together with Joachim Korff

The author:

Electrical engineering and economics graduate

Activities, experience:
- Electrician
- Project planning engineer
- Coordination of external companies
- International relocation, internal coordination
- Controller
- Production management
- ISO 9000 ff. Preparation for certification
- Company reorganization
- Preparation for IPO, in-house
- Management board assistant
- Lecturer for electrical engineering

Work for NGOs in:
- Afghanistan, site manager
- Rwanda, lecturer in electrical engineering
- Uganda, project manager

Publications in the field of tension between technology, organization and economics